F

"Lorilee lays the groundwork ᵢₒᵣ ₐₑₒᵣₑₐₛᵢₙ₉ ₜₕₑ ₜₑₙₐₑₙ₉ ₜₒ ᵣᵤₙ around without any meaning and to really start living our one beautiful life in this world with purpose and intention. In a world filled with noise, many of us are in dire need of coherence and silence in the mess. Whether it's simplifying your home or taking care of the self, [Lorilee] will help you find that much needed clarity."

—Nina, *Castles in the Air* blog

"From the moment I sat down to read . . . I was hooked. Literally, from page one I was already imagining what my home and life could look like if I took control of the 'stuff.' I was so inspired to hop up and start going through closets and yet I was glued to my seat wanting to read more. I was torn! While 'total minimalism' isn't for everyone, I think *anyone* can learn a lot about themselves from [this book]. I appreciated the positive approach that came with each step in simplifying. The book was clear and concise, direct but not judgmental, and I appreciated the focus on changing yourself first then leading by example. If you are looking for a great guide to simplifying your life or need a jump start to help clear out the clutter then [this book] is for you!"

—Jessy, *At Peace with Crazy*

"Lorilee is full of wisdom, but this isn't a lofty manifesto that leaves you wondering where to actually start. Instead, she offers tons of practical tips and ideas for actually simplifying—your stuff, your day-to-day life, and yourself!"

—Mandi, *Life Your Way*

". . . a must-have for anyone who wants to finally take control of all the 'stuff' in their homes and in their lives. Lorilee's book is inspiring, informational, and instructional without being preachy . . . and her writing style is friendly and fun. I have already used this book to declutter parts of my home and I'm so excited to keep going with it!"

—Maggie, *Midwest Sewing Girl*

Tidying Up
Your Life

**Declutter Your Home,
Streamline Your Schedule,
and Focus Your Mind**

Lorilee Lippincott

Skyhorse Publishing

Skyhorse Publishing books may be purchased in bulk at special discounts for sales promotion, corporate gifts, fund-raising, or educational purposes. Special editions can also be created to specifications. For details, contact the Special Sales Department, Skyhorse Publishing, 307 West 36th Street, 11th Floor, New York, NY 10018 or info@skyhorsepublishing.com.

Skyhorse® and Skyhorse Publishing® are registered trademarks of Skyhorse Publishing, Inc.®, a Delaware corporation.

Visit our website at www.skyhorsepublishing.com.

10 9 8 7 6 5 4 3 2 1

Library of Congress Cataloging-in-Publication Data is available on file.

Cover design by Daniel Brount

ISBN: 978-1-5107-5703-5

Printed in the United States of America

This book is dedicated to

my amazing husband, who has believed in me and taught me so much. He has been the support that has helped me try new things, and I can't imagine my life without him. Thanks, baby!

CONTENTS

Introduction   ix

3.

Stuff 3
Let's Start in the Closet   15
Now to the Kitchen   21
The True Beast   27
Hidden Out in the Open   37
Shelter   41
Continuing with Stuff Simplicity   45
Final Tip   49
Questions   51

2.

Space   57
Time   59
Drawing the Circle in the Sand   65
Money   73
Electronics   81
Simplify Sound   87
On the Plate and Under the Skin   89
Questions   95

1.

Self   101
The World as We Know It   103
Window to the World   107
Digging Deeper   111
Out of Body Simple   127
Questions   131

Stop.

Stop   135
My Journey   139
Ending Thoughts   144
Acknowledgments   145
Index   147

Introduction

This book is about stepping out of the crazy rat race and expectations our society creates. In this book I want to share with you our personal experiences, as well as what we have learned. I want to create a book that will offer some step-by-step help, as well as some ideals to guide your way.

Let's get something straight right away. This isn't a book to improve your bank statement or retirement plan, fix your house, or perfect your kids. This also isn't a book about being lazy, irresponsible with money, or not planning for the future. There are books out there for that and, frankly, most of them complicate life even more. I absolutely believe that within these pages there are secrets for success, but to start, we need to define what success really is. There are enough people out there who tell you that success is the money you have, the toys you have, the house you have, the résumé you have; but when it all comes down to it, maybe none of that really matters. Beyond that, these might not be areas that really matter to you. Maybe it is someone else's life you've been living and someone else's success you've been chasing.

This book will help clear out the craziness and clutter in your life and make room for simplicity. I believe that both of us, you and me, have the space in our lives—emotional and physical—to do what we really want to do and what we believe God wants us to do. We can't, however, come close to fitting in all the other expectations that weigh us down. There isn't room for it all. This is where the need for simple starts. I want a life that is full, challenging, and constantly growing; but I want *my* life—one that includes what *I* value as well as God's plan for *me*—not someone else's.

Am I the right person to write this book? Maybe, maybe not. I am sure there are others who have a better handle on life than me, but in these pages, I have written my journey and perspective because I know there are others out there struggling like me. I hope that it can help you. I also need this book to remind me. Heaven knows, I have a hard time remembering what I have learned.

I am a perfectionist. I can relate to the rest of you who struggle to be perfect and always try to do your best in everything. So often, striving for perfection is key to personal and business advancement and what society calls success, but it is the enemy of simplicity. I don't want to lose my perfectionism; I want to learn where it is beneficial to use, but also where "good enough" is best.

My road to simplicity started in the fall of 2010. Really, it started for fear of a breakdown. I am not a strong emotional person. There is only so much I can hold up in my life, though I'd been trying to hold up so much more. I just couldn't keep living the way I was living. Something had to change. My life wasn't bad; it was actually pretty "normal." But I wanted to fit more time in for writing, my kids, and my family, and I just couldn't figure out how to make it work. I was homeschooling my kids and felt like I wasn't able to put the time and energy I wanted into the process. I felt like I wasn't succeeding in any of the roles I was trying so hard to fill.

What We Did

My husband and I decided to cut back on our material belongings so there would be less for me to take care of in the house. Once we got going, we realized we wanted to get rid of most of our stuff and decided to move with our two kids—ages four and seven—into a small apartment that fit our new life better. Most people looked at us like we were crazy. I *felt* crazy. Who, in their right mind, would choose to trade a house for an apartment, especially with two small kids?

We didn't have what most people would consider a lot of stuff to begin with. I think we were probably fairly normal and my stuff has always been organized. For the most part, I knew what I had and I could find it. Though sometimes finding it took longer than it should. We had a 2,000-square-foot house with all the typical "junk."

So we started getting rid of stuff. There was a pile in the basement for Goodwill and a pile for garage sale. We gave stuff away to friends and filled the trash and recycle cans for weeks. We listed our extra furniture on Craigslist. Once the piles started, they just kept getting bigger. Truly, when we had our garage sale, I was embarrassed at the mass of stuff that had collected. It always looks like more when it is spread out on the lawn!

With stuff sold, or otherwise given away, we moved in May of 2011 into an apartment with a 14-foot U-Haul truck. I was so excited. It felt incredible to have less stuff to worry about.

Over the next summer, fall, and winter, we just kept getting rid of stuff. By the summer of 2012 we had shrunk even more and decided to move again to a smaller apartment so we could spend less on rent. This move was with a 10-foot U-Haul truck. It was the smallest truck they rent. The move from packing, moving, and unpacking took just over one day.

Honestly, it feels a bit like losing weight. Getting started is the hardest part. Once you begin seeing change it gets easier and easier to keep going. (I have to say it has gotten a bit addictive. But, before you call me crazy and give up on the book, hear me out.)

YOUR STORY

Stop right now. Close your eyes and picture how you want your life to look. If you don't know where to start, the questions below might help.

Picture your perfect life. Is it:

- ☐ Full of people or does it include only a few?
- ☐ Fast-paced or slow?
- ☐ Beach or mountain?
- ☐ Cozy or active?
- ☐ Loud or quiet?
- ☐ What is it centered on?
- ☐ What does it look, feel, smell, sound, or taste like?

There. That should be enough to start you off. Just close your eyes and dream a bit. Take three minutes or three hours. I will wait for you.

(Dream break)

Extra Information

In this book, I am going to use four terms that often can be used interchangeably, but they all mean slightly different things. Here is my dictionary-modified definition of these words:

> **Simple:** readily understood and performed. This isn't the same as easy. The task or the way might be hard, but the direction and the steps are clear.

> **Minimalist:** a style or technique that is characterized by extreme spareness and simplicity.

> **Intentional:** a thought-out and decided choice to act in a certain way.

> **Focused:** a state or condition permitting clear perception or understanding.

What I want to share with you in this book goes beyond material stuff. Sure, stuff is often the major obstacle, and it is the visible fix, but simplifying your life needs to go much deeper. Society has turned our life into *crazy* on so many levels that we really need to dissect who we are, how we think, how we act, and ask these simple questions:

- ☐ Is this what I want?
- ☐ Is this benefiting me?
- ☐ Why am I doing this?

So often we "just do" because it's habit, or because we grew up thinking we should. Just face it, there are too many things that fit in this category. There is no way to accomplish them all. Not only that, it could be a waste of a life. Let's create our own lives. My life and your life. Let's figure out what we really want to do, have, think, and what we want to be remembered for. And on top of all that, let's have fun; let's enjoy our lives. We each only get one!

Why am I starting with Part 3? Because this book follows the format of "3, 2, 1, Stop!" Instead of seeing this as a building book, think of it as a slowing book. Three steps on the journey to a simpler life.

Excited? Let's go!

Life Update

The very first edition of this book was originally written in 2012—so much has changed for me since then. I first started on a "Simple Living" or "Minimalist" journey late 2010. At that time I was thirty years old and my kids were seven and four. Now, when this new edition comes out, I will be forty and my kids will be sixteen and thirteen. Writing this book initially was a way to help me process the changes we were going through. Talking about it and sharing it with you was a way of both documenting that season of our lives as well as holding ourselves accountable to this new way of living.

My life isn't the same now as it is in these pages. However, I've kept most of the book the same because it is a complete picture of where we were at that point in our lives. It is where we were when I first wrote this book that lead to where we are now (but more of that later).

I wanted to keep the book the same and then also tell you about where we are now because it shows two different stages of simple living. Learning, stretching (or shrinking), and practicing minimalism at first is the hardest part. That is where I was when I first wrote this book and that might be where you are now.

With this edition I am also able to share with you where the journey took us. I can tell you that simple living isn't the destination but the beginning of what you can do and become. While I've decided to leave most of the book as it was originally published, I have added a chapter at the end to tell you about our journey since I originally wrote it.

I can also tell you that I had the romantic idea that I could make and control my own life. It is one of life's tensions in that this is both true and false. As a family, we did make a lot of uncomfortable and scary (at the time) choices because we were trying to be intentional and create our life. I believe this is always worth it. At the same time we didn't have full control—the life we have now is a combination of both realities.

It was exciting to re-read the book now, looking back. I feel like it's the writing of a different person. It's definitely a person I'd love to know and spend time with, but it doesn't feel like who I am now.

I'm excited for you as the reader. I wonder what kind of chapter you might add to your story ten years from now, sharing about the journey you are starting on now.

3.

Stuff

Ready!

Are you ready to stop *crazy* and allow *simple* to flow in? Doesn't that sound great? Let's start with the basics: the stuff you can see, the stuff that trips you up in the dark. This might seem like the most work, but as we get going, our stuff is not the worst habit we hold onto (but more on that later).

I am not here to help you organize your stuff. If when you dreamed up your perfect life in the introduction it included tons of color-coded totes and hours of sorting, then you have the wrong book. My ideal life has more beach and sunshine and no fancy labeled totes.

What Is "Stuff?"

To really understand the meaning of stuff, sometimes you need to move it. Do you remember moving into your current house? (Hopefully you do, otherwise your level of stuff might be dangerously high!) Remember hauling box after box up and down the stairs? Maybe you gave up moving yourself and paid someone to do it. Maybe you had some college kids hauling boxes for hours and hours. How long did it take you to pack? Unpack? Do you remember thinking to yourself, *What is all this stuff?* or *This can't all be mine!* or *Where did all this come from?* When you move, it's easier to see stuff for its true stuff-ness.

Doesn't stuff sound more like a master than a servant?

Stuff Demands:
- ☐ Moving
- ☐ Sorting
- ☐ Storing
- ☐ Maintaining
- ☐ Fixing
- ☐ Losing
- ☐ Hiding
- ☐ Disposing

That's a lot of hassle! Some things can dodge around the cycle several times before finally reaching disposing, only to start over again with a replacement or two! Now, there is definitely stuff worth having, but looking at this list and the time it represents, it screams at me to keep it to a minimum. Stuff is time consuming and expensive, no matter what color of tote it's in.

I'm not against stuff. I'm against the mass of stuff that seems to creep in and multiply like bunnies, stealing my time and my life.

It is sad, really, that our society needs to be on guard and almost wage a battle against stuff. There are people all over the world suffering from lack, who do not have the most basic needs, while we are so privileged that we need to bar the door against excess.

What I'm talking about has been called minimalism, or becoming a minimalist. It's a movement of brilliant people who question the societal norm of more, bigger, newer, shinier, and better, and decide that they don't need it, nor want to be controlled by it.

There is no set definition or list of stuff to have (or *not* have) to be a minimalist. A minimalist has the stuff they need and love. Nothing more.

Before we get to all the messy sorting, dream with me about what your life could be like if you only had what you needed and loved.

- ☐ Minimal shopping
- ☐ Minimal cleaning
- ☐ Minimal sorting
- ☐ Minimal hunting (for that thing you knew you had at one time but can't remember where you put it or when you had it last)
- ☐ Minimal moving
- ☐ Minimal tripping

Before you get worried, remember, you are the one in control of your stuff. No one says you have to get rid of the "blankie" or anything else. Minimalism is an intentional growing process. For our family, it started slowly and has continued as we have kept cutting down. At some point we may choose to have more stuff. The thing is that it is intentional control over stuff instead of being controlled and pushed around by it.

Minimalism with stuff began to appeal to me in the winter of 2010–2011. During this time, my husband got traveling construction work and we all packed up and went with him. To many people, travel for work can be a drag, but to us, it was an adventure. Between being self-employed and homeschooling, we were free to be spontaneous and go where we pleased. We loved our "move" five hours south for most of the winter months. It was during this time that the hubby and I were struggling with stress and schedules and generally being drained. The time spent down at our "away work" was almost like a vacation (okay, to me it was much more like a vacation because my husband actually did the work while I sat at the pool with the kids). It got us thinking:

- ☐ Why do we love our traveling work so much?
- ☐ Do we want to do this for a living?
- ☐ What is so different about this than our time at home?

Where we were traveling for work was no more exciting than our hometown. The five hours south had a nice ten-degree temperature increase which made the winter more bearable, but that wasn't really it. Then it all became much clearer—I had half my life back. We had no space to take care of in the hotel, only a few toys to put away, only a few clothes to wash, and only a few dishes. I know I sound like a complaining housewife, but taking care of all our stuff, all the kids' schoolwork, and managing the paper and computer work for the business required lots of time. Cutting out the house gave me time to think, read, dream, and recollect myself and my thoughts.

Unfortunately, we couldn't do the traveling thing for a living. The next and obvious question was, how can we make our life more like it was when we were traveling? How can we capture that sense of simple? The obvious answer was to cut out extra material stuff. When we were gone for all those months we didn't miss much. We were clothed, and the kids weren't fighting over toys (any more than normal). We joked that we should get rid of it all and drive away in our car. (Not sure where to, but it sounded great!) It was different when we came home and started sorting out what to get rid of. Looking at and holding things makes them harder to part with. Stuff I hadn't touched or remembered for months somehow regained its value.

The books were first; I don't know why. I love books, so maybe it was a bad place to start. I got rid of 80 percent of them. It was hard at first, but as I got rid of one or two, others became easier.

From the books we moved around the whole house. We got rid of 70 to 80 percent of what we owned.

I am excited to say that we did accomplish the simplifying of stuff, and you can too. Really, just getting started is the hardest part. It gets more fun as you go.

But first, some ground rules:

- ☐ **You are not your stuff and your stuff does not define you**
- ☐ **Your stuff is not your memories**
- ☐ **Your stuff is not your friends—they may have been with you or given it to you, but your friend will not vanish as a person if you get rid of the stuffed poodle or [insert your own random item here] they gave you**
- ☐ **Your stuff does not dictate your economic value in the world, your self-worth, or your importance**

There. You might have to read this list again, maybe a few times so it can really sink in. Different people struggle with different areas, but feel free to come back here if you get discouraged or distracted. Put up a sticky note on the mirror, whatever it takes: **I am more than my stuff!**

Before you dive in, it is *very* important to take a second and establish a system to minimize the continuing damage. I am all about efficiency and don't want you to do anything you don't have to. Stop creating more work for yourself. If you want to go through this simplification process, you need to put a stop to what enters the house. How? Let's go over some ways.

Mail and Other Papers

Paper comes into the home by the truckload with mail, work receipts, and kids' projects. Sort it immediately into these categories:

- ☐ File—a "to-file" pile is fine if it is in a clean organized spot, but it should just include what is going in the file, not envelopes or other trash.
- ☐ Trash—preferably recycle
- ☐ To Do—bills to pay, etc.

Purchases

Stop buying stuff! This might seem like a no-brainer, but this is hard. My weaknesses are sales, clearance, and bulk shopping. Yours might be something else. The deal is, over the next few weeks or months, the amount of "stuff" needs to shrink, so let's not make that harder. I have caught myself at the checkout (mostly at Target) with stuff in my cart just because it is "such a great deal" and had to pull it out at the last minute (I haven't always caught myself . . . but I remember my good moments). Here is my general rule for this:

Food—I will eat this in the next two (maybe three) weeks. This might mean buying a smaller size, and can't always be met, but it is a good starting point.

Stuff—I really, actually, truly need this (like we are running out of toilet paper) or I will need/use this up in the next three months. If it isn't needed or going to be used up, think hard on it, or sleep on it. This isn't a money thing. It's a stuff-accumulation thing.

If you are like me you are within minutes, or walking distance, from a store. If, by chance, there is a terrible storm, or terrorist attacks, FEMA only recommends having supplies in your house for three days, so shopping with the above guidelines should be fine. Never will you need a year's supply of TP for an emergency. (I had that once—found a great deal.) So, if something worse happens, and you are stuck in your house for three weeks, you can sue the government. Just kidding.

So, now that you have cut down the amount of stuff coming in, you can start sorting through what you already have. Ready? I am so excited for you! Really, I am. It is daunting at first, but it will get easier, I promise.

I want you to write out all the "areas" of your stuff. It might look something like this:

- ☐ Kitchen
- ☐ Garage
- ☐ Upstairs bathroom
- ☐ Laundry room
- ☐ Spare bedroom

- ☐ Car (hopefully there isn't much here, but if you have kids like me, sometimes it doubles as an extra walk-in closet)
- ☐ Storage unit
- ☐ Mom's attic
- ☐ Bookshelf in office

Make this your master list, and I encourage you to break it down as much as possible into smaller areas, maybe separating out closets in rooms. Now that you have a list you can read, touch, and hold, it can become your to-do list to go through and "minimalize," or simplify. Unless you are already living a pretty simple lifestyle, this isn't a list you are going to tackle in a day. (Though, maybe, down the road, it could all be gone through in a few hours; that is where we are at now.) This isn't the same as cleaning; this is deeper. This is a process that could take weeks, months, years (hopefully not, but you get the idea).

Now, pick an easy spot and get started. I started with my bookshelf, but you can start wherever you want. This is how it is going to work:

First
Everything gets pulled out.

Second
Sort into five piles:

- ☐ Trash
- ☐ Give away (donate or to a friend)
- ☐ Sell
- ☐ Keep—put back
- ☐ Not sure

Why have a "not sure" pile? Having this pile helps you keep going when you run into something that you just aren't sure about. Don't let an item stop you; throw it in this pile.

Third

Go through the "not sure" pile and decide which of the other four piles the items will go in. Alternatively, you can put the "not sure" pile in a box and label it with the date. If it stays in the garage for six months (or whatever length of time you decide) without being needed, it graduates to the sale or giveaway pile. Most of my "not sure" stuff gets put with the "keep" stuff originally, but later, when I have gone through it again, it gets pulled for sale or giveaway. This isn't supposed to be a painful or stressful time, but a freeing time. Don't get rid of something that you don't feel comfortable getting rid of.

As I was sorting, it helped to ask myself "Is it replaceable?" Is this something I could get again easily, for not very much money, if I do decide I need it again? For example, a book that I could find at the library, or buy used off Amazon for a few dollars if I decide I want to read it again, is "safe" enough to get rid of. Something that is cheap, or especially bulky that you aren't sure you are going to use or need is great for this. Get rid of it, and you can always get another one or borrow one later, if necessary. Keeping things "just in case" could derail your whole simplifying process, so don't fall into that trap.

The next few chapters go over several areas of the house that I want to deal with specifically. They are not in a particular order. Feel free to read in whatever order you choose to work in. If you're looking for more guidance, I recommend checking out *The Joy of Less*, by Francine Jay. Great book!

Are you ready with the trash, giveaway or donate, sell, and a "not sure" box or pile? Let's go!

Let's Start in the Closet

I could give recommendations on how many shirts or black socks you should have, or the necessity of a black A-line skirt (or the male equivalent), but there are already lots of those lists out there. What is going to make the best minimalist closet for you is a personal decision, because it's about your life—what you wear day-to-day.

Before you start going through your closet, make an "ideal closet wish-list." Write down how many of each clothing item you want your wardrobe to have. For example, you might decide you need five short-sleeved shirts, two pairs of jeans, and so on. It is important to make your wish-list *before* you look in your closet because, once you look in your closet, one of two things will happen:

1. You will decide you need more clothes because you don't want to get rid of what you have.

2. You will decide you don't need specific things because they are not in your closet.

You can take a shopping spree after you go through your closet and fill in anything you might still be missing from your list. However, chances are greater that there is considerably more excess than there are holes when you compare your list to your actual closet. You are going to create your ideal closet!

You will need to find one more box or bag for the closet sorting; this one will be for storage.

Now, Pull Everything Out!

The closet is a place where stuff seems to multiply. Without proper taming it is wild, scary, and dangerous, so get all the way to the back and bottom. Now, with the pile you created:

1. Remove everything that isn't appropriate for the current season.

2. Remove everything that isn't appropriate for the current phase of life (i.e., prom dress, unless you are planning to attend).

3. Remove everything that doesn't fit. Too big or too small, get it out.

4. Remove everything you love, but don't wear.

5. Remove everything you don't like and never wear.

6. Remove anything you shouldn't wear 'cause it's ugly, even if it is comfortable. Bye-bye!

7. Remove everything that doesn't fit right. It might "fit" from #3, but it just doesn't hang right, bunches funny, or is too long or too short for your body shape. This is the item that's never comfortable, that you're always pulling at or feels funny when you wear it.

8. Definitely remove everything that is stained or torn or missing buttons or is in any way broken.

Separate What You Removed into the Following Piles:

☐ **Store:** This might be for a favorite memory item, out-of-season clothes (that you like and will wear when that season comes around), clothes that will fit soon (like in the next three months . . . realistically, not dreaming). Also include stuff you aren't sure about getting rid of yet. If you do want or need that item you can pull it out of storage. Or the next time you sort, it will be easier to get rid of, seeing that you have clearly not used it.

☐ **Donate:** The beautiful sweater you never wear but is just too pretty to throw away will look great on someone else. It will be treasured and maybe help some poor soul get a job or save a life, or whatever story you want to tell yourself. It is easier to get rid of some items if we see a new life for them instead of an end.

☐ **Sell:** Some stuff might work to sell, but my experience with clothes is that it isn't worth the hassle of selling unless it is high end and almost new, and can be sold at a consignment shop.

- ☐ **Toss:** Yep, there is probably some of this.
- ☐ **Is there stuff to fix?:** You can make a fix pile, but make sure that 1) you know how to fix it; 2) you actually will fix it; 3) when it is fixed you will like it, fit in it, and will actually wear it.

Okay, Now Let's Tackle What Is Left of the Pile (Hopefully Much Less)!

Take some time to compare this with the wish-list you made earlier. Chances are you have many more items in particular categories than you said you wanted. For example, you might have said you wanted five short-sleeved shirts and you have twenty. In this case, I recommend one of two things:

1. Store the extra and pull out as needed when others wear out or stain. This works like a little storage-closet-mall.

2. Pick the best and donate or sell the rest.

The best option is probably a combination of both. You probably don't need to store fifteen extra short-sleeved shirts to use over four or more years. The point is that the extra isn't sitting in your closet. In the example above, only five short-sleeved shirts will be put back in the closet. That's it!

I can't tell you exactly what to have in your closet, but I tackled my closet and cut it down dramatically. Let me share with you my current list. You are welcome to use this list as a starting point and modify as needed.

My Minimalist Closet

- 3 church dresses
- 1 pantsuit
- 1 pair of khaki dress pants
- 2 button-up shirts
- 1 sweater
- 1 light coat
- 1 pair of jeans
- 1 "slouchy" pants for around the house or to sleep in
- 1 yoga pants (I love these things)
- 1 pair of shorts
- 2 dressy-ish shirts
- 1 bathing suit
- Enough undergarments for 8 or 9 days (I will spare you the details)
- 5 solid short-sleeve shirts
- Running/walking shoes for everyday use
- 2 pairs of black shoes
- 1 pair cute brown flats
- 1 pair black boots
- 1 pair strappy sandals
- 2 purses (1 small, 1 big)

It looks like a long list typed out, but it doesn't feel or look like much in the closet. Nothing gets stuck at the bottom of the drawer. Everything is easy to use and easy to find.

Kids' and men's wardrobes work about the same. All four of us share one closet in our apartment now.

Wow! If you're anything like I was, the closet should look a bit different. Congratulations! Maybe, the once-too-small closet looks a lot roomier!

Now to the Kitchen

The kitchen was a big problem of bulk for me. Not only did I have lots of cooking utensils and pans, but I loved buying food in bulk.

Why do manufacturers need to make different bulky tools for every different kind of food?

- ☐ Pizza oven
- ☐ Quesadilla maker
- ☐ Snow cone machine
- ☐ Fondue pots
- ☐ Grilled cheese sandwich press
- ☐ Popcorn popper
- ☐ Smoothie maker
- ☐ Avocado slicers
- ☐ Pasta measuring tools
- ☐ And a host of others

If we are just trying to cook basic food in our home kitchens, the retail establishment will argue that we need a truckload of kitchen gadgets to make it happen. This is not true. Sure, some of these gadgets might be great for their one task, but if I own them all, I won't be able to find them the one or two times a year when I would actually use them.

When I cleared my kitchen of extra gadgets, I tried to gauge their value by the amount I actually used them and by their size. I love baking mini desserts and I had lots of different mini dessert pans (cheesecakes, tarts, angel food cake, bread pans, and more). I loved the idea of miniature, individually-sized pans, but I hardly used them. So I got rid of most of them. Then I got rid of the snow cone maker. Yes, we used it more often, but it was this huge bulky contraption that took up half a shelf. We kept the ice cream maker, instead, because we love it more and use it all the time. Now the kids will just have to have ice cream instead of snow cones, poor dears.

I also discovered that I had too many pans, pots, mixing bowls, and measuring cups (just to name a few). I decided how many I really needed and got rid of the extra. So now, on occasion, when I am doing lots of cooking I have to wash a few things between recipes. So far, this hasn't been the end of the world. Between gadgets I didn't need and duplicate items, I got rid of at least half of my kitchen things.

Does that help a little? Every kitchen looks a bit different, but in my experience, most people have a collection of gadgets and tools that are rarely, if ever, used. Some may even still be brand-new.

If you are afraid to part with an item and fear that you may desperately need it in the future, ask yourself these questions:

- ☐ Would something else work?
- ☐ How expensive would it be to replace?

Now, you have the non-edible part of the kitchen sorted into piles of sale, giveaway, and trash. There might be a store pile, but there shouldn't be too much here. If you don't use it, you might not need it. Do you really need to eat off different dishes at Christmas? Maybe? But probably not.

Edible Items

Now for the food! I love food. Sometimes it is necessary and easy to buy in bulk (especially when the price is right). But, at one time a few years ago, my basement had more than thirty boxes of cereal and more than twenty bags of corn chips. I had found the cereal and chips for $1 apiece on sale; I couldn't pass it up! Not only did I have bulk food stashed in the basement, I had it stored in the kitchen, I had a full deep freeze, and I had some in the spare bedroom closet. Looking back, it was a bit insane—you can think I am crazy now if you want. For the record, it was all organized and not past the due date.

The problem becomes the need for space, the need for organization, and using it before it goes stale, or moldy. I went through it often, which took a lot of time.

Strategies for cutting down food are different. There might be some extra stuff you can sell or donate, but the majority of it will be tossed or used up.

The fact that food is still in your house doesn't mean it will be eaten. Often it is just more junk lying around. Keeping food until it goes bad is not economical; it is a waste of space and time.

It needs to be trashed or removed if it is:

1. Past its due date

2. A spice that has been in the cupboard for longer than you can remember

3. Food you have hung onto for ages but never touched (if this is not past a due date, donate it to the food bank)

The second method to controlling the mass of food is to eat what you have, by planning meals around it, instead of buying more. This is a basic budgeting principle, but actually doing it takes some practice. Go through the cupboards and make a menu for the next week, or the next two weeks, focusing on what is there that needs to be used up. I try to keep most food in my kitchen for no more than a few weeks.

Salt and spices are usually not used up in two weeks. But I have also learned that I don't need a huge spice cabinet stocked with stuff I hardly use. I just end up holding it until it expires and pitching it. That is a waste. So, now I have just a handful of spices I really like, and I try to buy them in amounts that are manageable.

It took us months of eating and preparing meals around what we had to use up our stash. It worked wonders for the food budget! It's kind of like when you are about to leave on vacation, or about to move. You just buy the food that you will use right away, and you make sure to use the stuff you have on hand. You can eat this way all the time; it just takes practice.

What if you had a smaller fridge or smaller kitchen space? What would you keep? How would you eat? Often we collect and fill the space we have instead of focusing on what we actually need. Doesn't a small kitchen with favorite foods, and fresh foods, sound much more appealing? It sure does to me. We will be continuing this topic in Part 2 where we will talk about how to simplify what we eat. This will help simplify food kept in the kitchen even more.

The True Beast

How's it going? Excited yet? Finding some space? Now that we have gone through some of the personal areas, let's plunge into one of the biggest and scariest battles—kids' toys.

Kids' toys are crazy! They breed like rabbits, and they come out of everywhere. It's often hard to really know the true size of the beast, because they spread out and hide all over the place. For this reason, the first thing to do with this animal is to get it caged. Find a spot to collect them all. I used the kids' bedrooms.

Find the toys—all the toys:

- ☐ Kids' rooms
- ☐ Living room
- ☐ Den
- ☐ Playroom
- ☐ Car
- ☐ Under things (parents' bed, refrigerator, stove, piano)
- ☐ Storage
- ☐ Bath toys

- ☐ Kitchen
- ☐ Outside (these might not be able to come inside to join the others, but they need to be corralled in one spot as well)
- ☐ Any other places they might hide

I am not saying that they need to stay there. It is good to have a few toys in different places, but for this exercise, the true size and amount needs to be dealt with while they are together. What and how many do the kids actually own?

Sort with Kids or Without?

This is an interesting debate and probably depends on the personalities of the kids, their ages, and other factors, but a combination will probably work best. For us, I did most of the cleaning out and sorting of the kids' toys (ages seven and four), but they were involved after the initial taming, and are involved in the upkeep.

This is what I would recommend. Without the kids, remove:

- ☐ Anything broken
- ☐ Anything missing enough pieces that it isn't fun anymore
- ☐ Anything that drives you, as a parent, crazy (yep, you know what fits in here)
- ☐ Anything they haven't played with in ages
- ☐ Anything not age appropriate for them (younger or older)

- ☐ Any duplicates that aren't necessary (kids love lots of stuffed animals, but are fifty necessary, or do they need two train sets that can't work together?)

These need to be sorted between trash, giveaway, and sell. There might be some storage, a memory (favorite baby toy), or toys that they haven't grown into yet. But there shouldn't be too much storage from this first clean out. This process could easily take half, or more, of the toys out of the collection.

After I had cleaned all this stuff out of my kids' rooms in the spring of 2011, I let my kids help organize the rest. We were planning our move to an apartment and were getting ready for a garage sale. Since everything left was in good condition, I let them decide what they might like to sell (and I let them keep the money, because they were saving for a Kindle). They ended up wanting to get rid of way more than I thought they would!

Often people have told me that their kids will never decide to get rid of anything, or sell anything. This is probably true for most kids, because it is also true for most parents. I intentionally put toys near the end of the section on paring down because kids need to see their parents make changes first. If they see you:

- ☐ Going through your stuff, reducing it, and enjoying the outcome

- ☐ Talking about how the things you are getting rid of are helping other people who don't have as much
- ☐ Planning what you are going to do with the money after you sell your stuff

... they will follow your lead. It has to be a change in the parents before it will be an accepted change in the child. It might take some time before the kids really embrace it but letting them be involved in the process could make all the difference. So, after the initial parent sweep you can go through the rest with your kids. Use the donate, sell, and store pile. It might work well if you set rules for what can stay in the room, but let them decide which pile to put the extra stuff in. They might want to keep and store a bunch more than you do, but they might decide to get rid of more than you would.

Here are some examples of rules for giving kids control, while keeping the outcome clear:

- ☐ "You can keep five stuffed animals. Which ones would you like to keep?"
- ☐ "We don't have enough room in your bedroom to have A as well as B and still have room for you to play. Which one do you like better?"
- ☐ "This is the box we can keep your favorite crafts in. Do you want to pick out which crafts you want to keep? Let's put them in this box."
- ☐ "Do you want to give some of these other crafts away? I know Grandma might like this one." (Just

like us, giving away is often much easier than throwing away.)

I much prefer this positive perspective. The goal of cleaning out the kids' room is that they have a clean (and easy to clean) space with toys that encourage creative play and imagination. We want a room kids will be excited to run into by themselves, with siblings, or with friends, and get lost for hours playing games that they will talk about over dinner and continue in their dreams. This is the environment we are trying to create! It is about creating an outcome, not about denying or cutting back.

Here are some great toys for kids. Like the wardrobe, cleaning out might leave some gaps that can be filled in with better things they do need. You can modify for age and personality of kids:

- ☐ Art stuff—This can get out of hand. Remove all the finished projects, the broken crayons, and dried-up markers. They need a clean space to work and a few tools that are easy to get out. (Few = not overwhelming.)
- ☐ Dolls or stuffed animals—These are what my kids play with the most. This is where they make up story lines and act them out for a long time. All their stuffed animals have names and need to be "taken care of."
- ☐ Construction stuff—Blocks, LEGO, Lincoln Logs, etc. However, they don't need a set of each. If they have all these (or other combinations) they get mixed

up together and kids get frustrated when they try to build a castle with a combination of different pieces that don't fit together.

☐ Dress-up clothes—These don't need to be fancy, just durable and not too specific. Toys and dress-up clothes are better if they can be made into several different characters. For example, a Snow White dress or Spiderman suit really only works with those characters, but a fancy dress or a plain cape can be made into lots of different princesses or superheroes. They are free to make up their own names and story lines.

☐ Active toys—Bike (and safety equipment), baseball and glove, swimming floaters. They don't need balls and gear for every sport, but they need the right, good quality stuff to encourage them in some activities they love.

☐ Games and puzzles—These need to be age appropriate and simple. Seriously, some of the best games are the games that have been around forever with simple rules, simple board (no batteries), or even just playing cards. Get rid of games that are more work than they are worth.

If you haven't noticed, most toys sold now don't fit on this list. It can be tricky to find gifts for kids that fit on this list and that they don't already have. This is a retail-created problem with gifts being almost an everyday expectation. Stuff now seems to be a reward for Christmas, birthday, report card, obedience in the store, and almost every day for just "being." No wonder the toy beast is so big.

I really enjoy and recommend *Simplicity Parenting* by Kim John Payne. He has some great ideas for what toys kids need. Notice that educational toys aren't on this list. Payne doesn't think much of them and I haven't found any educational toys that really help my kids. Since they have both started school, they often use their new knowledge in their play. Isn't that what knowledge is supposed to do, make our lives easier by helping us do what we want to do? So they don't need special math toys or special letter toys (a simple set of letters is nice, but I think the fancy talking big stuff is too much). One game that utilizes the knowledge they gain from school is "Store." They will create their own stores (parents can definitely help), price stuff, and sell it to their friends. They will start making signs and writing notes if the paper and pens are around. Knowledge will fit and grow in their world as they learn and use it.

We know it, but it's easy to forget. Children don't need stuff. Children need:

- ☐ Love
- ☐ Time and experiences
- ☐ Room for creativity
- ☐ Food, shelter, and education

That's about it.

My kids have very little and have kept simplifying over the last eighteen months now. I wanted to share with you what they have. Every family is different; this list is just an example. There are many ways to adopt these principles.

This Is What's in My Kids' Room:

- ☐ Book basket—My kids have about thirty books each that they chose to keep. They can have ten each in their book basket and the rest are stored up in their closet. Whenever they want, they can trade books out. It isn't a punishment to keep them up there, just a way to help them keep stuff neater.
- ☐ Box of cars and little toys of my son's.
- ☐ Dress-up clothes—They both have a few dress-up clothes in one tub.
- ☐ Box of Fisher-Price Trio blocks—Both kids love these.
- ☐ Small box of LEGO—my son is just starting to get into these.
- ☐ Box of K'NEX—It is a bit above my son, but sometimes they both really get into it.
- ☐ Box of Barbie stuff—My daughter has really cut back on the Barbie stuff. She now just has a few dolls and a few different outfits for them.
- ☐ Doll stuff—same as the Barbies, my daughter has cut down what her dolls own to match how she sees our family. We have minimalist dolls!
- ☐ Organizers for their clothes—they don't have many clothes and we don't have dressers in our house because I hate how they take up floor space and create another top to collect stuff. For kids, I worry that a dresser will fall over on them.

- ☐ Art stuff—they have access to colored pencils, pens, crayons, and plain paper. We have a box of craft supplies when we want to tackle a bigger art project in homeschool.
- ☐ Puzzles and games—We have a small selection of each. These are great family activities and help them use their reading and math skills.
- ☐ Bikes and helmets, scooters, soccer ball, basketball, and some pool toys.

That's it. Sure, they can still make a pretty big mess with all this stuff, but it is a mess they can clean up (though often still with complaining and fighting, because they are kids). Will this always be their list? Probably not. By the time you read this they might have more or less; this is where we are happy now.

Do they miss their other toys or ask for more? Not really. This is surprising to me. Often they talk about what they used to have, but not about missing it, or wanting it back; it is just a fact and a memory. We don't have a TV and we, as parents, don't have much stuff. I think that is a lot of the reason they don't ask for stuff all the time. Sure, ask them what they want for their birthday or Christmas and they are more than able to come up with a list. But day-to-day, or walking through the store, there isn't nagging or battles. This is possible when you change yourself first, and then ask the kids to follow your example.

Happy sorting!

Hidden Out in the Open

I wanted to do a section on furniture. This is something people often overlook as they sort and simplify their belongings. The funny thing about furniture is that it isn't really needed, either.

What! Not Needed?

Hear me out. Really, furniture is needed to fill the space in our house/apartment, but we also look for a house/apartment that will hold all our furniture. Does that seem like a recipe for disaster? Considering the fact that houses and living spaces just keep getting bigger, I think it is.

There is probably an argument against these, but furniture that I (and probably most of the developed world) think is most important is:

☐ Something to sleep on—bed.
☐ Something to sit on—chair or sofa. If you want people to sit with you, you need more than one.

That is about it. Sure, some people want something to eat at, but not everyone. Because we have two small kids, a table is pretty important for us, but for others it might not be.

So where does all the other furniture come in?

☐ To fill up space and create "living space" in each room
☐ To hold our stuff

For example, how many chairs do you need? Well, often that depends on how many rooms you have because people might want to sit down in many different rooms. Want to read or play in more than one room? You need more furniture.

So with more and more stuff and with more and more space, we end up "needing" more and more furniture. This is kind of ironic because furniture is the biggest and bulkiest "stuff" that we have. Often cutting down stuff is better accomplished by getting rid of one piece of furniture than going through a whole stack of books, volume wise. If you have already been going through several areas of your house, you might already realize that a few pieces of furniture aren't as important as you thought before. Why keep the extra dresser if there is almost nothing left in it?

So, go through your furniture with the same fine-tooth comb as you have gone over other areas, asking if each item should be trashed, donated, or sold because it isn't worth the space it takes up in your house. After going through all your rooms, and now the furniture, maybe a smaller space would work out better for you as well. Who knew!

Shelter

Humans need food, water, and shelter. Yes, we need a house. But how much shelter do we need? Since the beginning of recorded time, it seems people have always wanted more space, more stuff, and bigger houses. Poor people had little shacks and rich people lived in castles, or the equivalent mix based on time or location. Now seems to be the first time that people seem to be questioning this and coming up with the idea that maybe bigger isn't better.

Gregory Paul Johnson wrote in *Put Your Life on a Diet: Lessons Learned from Living in 140 Square Feet* about living very comfortably (by choice) in what most would consider a tiny space. YouTube star Felice Cohen shows her ninety-square-foot apartment in Manhattan's Upper West Side. A bit of Googling shows that it is almost a new fad or competition to see how comfortably and fancy a person can live in the smallest space.

Lots of this came about from an environmental concern because considerable energy was being used to heat, cool, and light huge houses. The lack of space in the cities has also made people get creative. Now minimalism is just another great reason for a smaller space.

Don't I Need to Own a Home?

This isn't an automatic "yes" anymore. It used to be that owning a home was much better financially, but the world is changing. We have chosen to rent (we still own our home and rent it out as well, so maybe that is the best of both worlds) for these reasons.

1. A wise house investment, one that will hold its value and resell easily, is more square feet than I feel I need to live in. Just ask anyone trying to sell a small 800-square-foot single-family house with two bedrooms. There is almost no market for them at all. Sure, it might be a great deal to buy, but if you can't sell it later, it isn't a good investment.

2. Houses require lots of upkeep that I don't want crowding my simple life. I don't want to spend time and money keeping up my section of green space. I don't want to spend hours cleaning (or money paying someone to clean) just so I can have more rooms. I don't want to change that many light bulbs or wash that many windows.

3. A bigger space fills up with stuff much more easily.

4. It is much cheaper to have less space; cheaper rent, cheaper utilities, and a cheaper space to furnish.

5. Moving is *way* cheaper when you don't add selling or buying to the process. Selling or buying a house costs tens to hundreds of thousands of dollars and is often a huge source of stress. Houses can also depreciate over the short term or sit on the market for months or longer, causing even greater expense and stress. Moving often, for work or by choice, is a part of our society I see increasing, not going away.

Saving money for the future is very important, but owning a house isn't necessarily the way to do it. It can be a pretty poor way. With a thirty-year mortgage, the first several years pay very little down on principal, so that often, when people sell in five years or less, they lose money after paying real estate fees. That is on top of the extra you paid to own instead of renting a smaller space. If you can rent something smaller for less money, and invest the extra in other areas, you will end up much better in the long run.

Continuing with Stuff Simplicity

Now you have (hopefully) really cut down on stuff that has been stealing your time and energy. You are getting excited about your home being better and happier with less stuff. The kids are on board, and maybe you've actually shrunk your living space without leaving yourself feeling crammed in. *Ah! Happy sigh!*

However, the work is not over. Minimalizing stuff is a continual process. This surprised me. Last spring, we went through all our stuff in painful detail so we could move to our apartment. I thought that after we went through it once most of the work would be done. But I discovered that more and more stuff that I originally thought was necessary, I now wanted to get rid of. Several more times in the last few months, I've gone through our stuff and found more that we could trash, donate, and sell.

It is almost a competition, or status, in some circles of minimalism to get down to owning 100 (or fewer) things. This is refreshingly countercultural. Since we run several self-employment businesses and homeschool two children, I am quite sure we won't be able to get down to 100 things. I'm not even sure if we want to. However, after our last move to our one-bedroom apartment I realized: *If I wanted to, I could actually count our belongings now. I could count that high, all in one day!*

I haven't actually done it yet, and I'm not sure it's the best use of a day, but it is fun to realize that I could.

How much stuff does a person actually need? That is a very living and movable concept. When you read this we might have more, but based on our past years' experience, we will probably have less. Who knows? Ten years from now, my dream is that we will have just the right amount of stuff. The same with twenty years and fifty years from now.

What I know is, keeping the amount of stuff I own lower makes my life simpler and easier.

What I recommend and have done ever since we started the process, is have a spot in your house or apartment for the two piles: donate and sell. Whenever I am cleaning, or sorting, or picking up, and I find something I am not sure is worth its weight, space, or time to put away in our house, I know where to put it. We make a Goodwill run or post on Craigslist whenever necessary.

Isn't it terrible living in a small space like an apartment with kids?

I get this a lot. Really, we love apartment living. But having very little stuff is definitely something that has to happen first. Otherwise it would be very easy to feel cramped.

Our apartment is never clean when the kids are here, there is just too little space, and they are always messing something up. However, it is never very messy either. Every inch of space is used all the time. There isn't space for dirt, dust, or junk, to collect anywhere. Picking up with a small space and few things is quick but constant.

Final Tip

Clear off horizontal spaces. Horizontal spaces should be clear (or almost clear).

Just picture a house with clean countertops, only a fresh flower in a vase in the middle of the table, nothing on the TV or end tables, and maybe just the most recent copy of your favorite magazine on the coffee table (if you actually need the coffee table . . . I don't have one, they often just collect stuff). Now walk into the bedroom, the bed is made and only has pillows with shams (not piles of decorative pillows and extra blankets), the table by the bed has just a clock, and the dresser (if you have one) has nothing on it. The floor doesn't have anything extra on it but maybe a decorative, soft rug.

Are you starting to picture it? Just writing about it (while the floor at my feet is being covered with blocks by my little angel) is relaxing. Doesn't it sound like a place to come home to, to hang out with guests, or just enjoy by yourself? This is not necessarily the absence of stuff, this is just keeping the horizontal spaces and the areas in view stuff-free. The eye can travel around the room without tripping over everything and getting overwhelmed. Ah, bliss.

Questions

Should I garage sale, donate, or sell stuff some other way? How do I know which thing to put where?

This goes with your personality, and, maybe, your time more than anything. Amazon works well for books. Ebay for some collectibles. But both take time and may not be worth it for what you get paid in the end. I sold some recent textbooks easily on Amazon, but other books I didn't even try.

I haven't found it worth my time to try and sell clothes. The pricing and sorting takes so long and I have never really had success. No matter how cheaply I price something it needs just the right person with the same taste, and size, who is looking for that specific thing. That person might never come to the garage sale (or consignment shop).

We sold lots of stuff at our garage sale and, for bigger stuff, on Craigslist. Our garage sale had household stuff, kids' toys, extra kitchen stuff, and we held it for one day only. At the end of the day, we sold the rest for $50 to a junk collector guy who was going to take it and try to resell it.

What if my husband/wife doesn't agree with the idea of simplifying?

You can only change yourself, and although minimalism and simplifying are great, marriage and family relations are more important. My advice would be to change your thinking and your stuff, and live out the difference instead of trying to nag or get rid of their stuff as well. People are more important than stuff (or a lack of stuff).

What if I get rid of too much? Or not enough? How do I know?

This is tough. I would say don't get rid of anything you aren't comfortable with getting rid of yet. As I shared above, I have gone through several times and gotten rid of more and more. I found that once I got rid of the least exciting, useful, loved things, other things took their spot at the bottom and were easier to get rid of.

Now, if you don't feel comfortable getting rid of anything but you really want to cut back, you need to do some more thinking and soul searching.

If you are afraid of getting rid of too much (you might be right on track!), just make sure that what you get rid of, if you might need it again, is replaceable for a reasonable amount of money. I got rid of my table and chairs right away, and I am not sure why. It might not have been the smartest move, but I was excited and it helped snowball the whole process. Getting rid of bigger furniture makes big dents in the total amount of stuff and it inspires you to keep going.

Now on to other areas that need sorting and simplifying.

2.

Space

Now you have minimized your stuff and are living in a tranquil, beautiful spot. The house is clean and uncluttered with light and space everywhere. At the least, it's becoming that way in your head, which is the most important first step. I am excited for you!

However, stuff is only the beginning of truly minimizing, simplifying, and living intentionally. Our lives can continue to be crazy if we simplify only the tangible. The truth is that where, what, how, and why we do everything we do makes a big difference in our reality. Our home space can be simple while our lives continue being crazy.

I am going to talk about seven different areas of life that get crazy and crowd in on the beauty of simplicity. As you read through this section I want you to think:

My life is mine.
I am responsible for it.
If I don't like it, I am the one to change it.

Far too many people try to blame others, their past, upbringing, luck (or lack of it), and anything else they can for what is wrong in their lives. They believe that problems come from something outside themselves. The truth is that no one has a perfect life, this isn't a perfect world, and life definitely isn't fair. The beauty of being human is that we can take steps to change and improve our lives. No one else is going to do this for you; you have to put in the work.

While you may not have control over all of these seven areas, I bet you have control over most of them, and taking control where you can is an empowering start.

So, sit down in your cozy chair in your simple, uncluttered, clean room with a cup of something fancy and join me as we go through Part 2.

Time

Life has gotten faster and faster, and schedules have gotten crazier and crazier. A forty-hour work week sounds like a vacation, and some find much needed "vacations" on their sick bed almost inviting. I have been there. Thirty-two hours of work on a to-do list in a twenty-four-hour day just doesn't work.

Why is life so much more hectic today? We no longer need to plow the fields by hand, milk the cows, or sew our own clothes, and yet somehow we have less time to sit. I love reading the Little House series by Laura Ingalls Wilder to my kids. It creates a picture of what life was like years ago. Sure, life was hard, but during rainy or winter days, they had that time to sit by the fire at night and sing, talk, or play. Technology has helped us overcome those "inefficient" moments now, and life goes on 24-7 all year long.

Most families don't have any idea what sitting by the fire for the evening is like—they don't even have the time to sit down together for a meal. Many are eating in the car more than the dining room. This just isn't right.

This isn't just about families and good parenting; this isn't just about kids needing to relax; this isn't just about the need for time as a couple. All these are important! But even without all these responsibilities you need to cut back for your own selfish good. No one can keep this pace up.

Somehow, I have a hard time seeing our ancestors using planners to make sure everything was tightly scheduled and that it all fit.

- ☐ An Egyptian pulling out his planner to see if he can fit in a trip to the Nile between pyramid building.
- ☐ Columbus heading back to the captain's cabin to consult his planner and see when a good meeting time would be to talk to the crew.
- ☐ Native Americans carrying planners around strapped to the bottom of their bows to make sure they don't hunt too long and miss something back at camp.
- ☐ Laura's mom with a little planner tucked in her apron to make sure she can fit butter-making in between checking the chickens and weeding the garden.

It all sounds crazy, but today, people have planners everywhere and use them like a lifeline. When work was so hard, it wasn't near as crazy. So, now that our lives have been made easier with time-saving inventions, we are facing relational and emotional breakdowns and a whole host of stress-related diseases.

This doesn't have to be the case, but I agree it's hard to fight against, maybe even harder than the "stuff monster."

So, grab a pen and paper.

Just like with the material stuff, you need to sort what you have. Make out a weekly calendar of how you spend your time. All of it. Include time driving, on Facebook, or anything else that takes your time. This isn't a time to decide if it is good or not; this is just to collect it all and figure out where it goes.

Don't look at this list as a tool for organizing your life in order to get more productivity out of it. There may be room for that, but this isn't that kind of book. Not all time has to be productive! This has been a revelation and a challenge for me. To simplify and de-stress there needs to be "unproductive" relaxing time.

With this list, we are looking for the de-stressing time. It is a deliberate, efficient, and effective use of your time to pull back and do nothing.

So, the goal of the calendar is to figure out how to cut out/free up some of your time. Here are some ideas:

1. I once read that for kids (and I think adults would benefit as well) a family shouldn't have more than two weeknights with activities per week. This

includes kids' programs, meetings, working late, shopping, all of it. For the week, three nights should just be at home.

2. Limit work hours (this is a free country and it is possible to do). Depending on your work, this can be really hard and might not work every day, but deciding how many hours you are willing to give your employer and doing everything you can to keep it there will make a difference. Is all your time at work as effective as it could be? Are there responsibilities that could be passed on to someone else or eliminated? Often, work becomes habit and the need to look busy, overworked, and valuable is the reason for extra hours more than actual necessity. My husband and I struggle with limiting work hours. We're self-employed in the construction field and it should give us full control over our schedule, but there is always work to do. We have worked hard at setting limits in our business, but it is something we need to keep working at.

3. Cutting material stuff that takes your time (if you haven't already done that in Part 3). Hopefully the whole process of sorting and organizing has opened up a bunch of your time with less cleaning, sorting, organizing, and hunting.

4. Delegate. Depending on where you are financially and your priorities it might work well to hire help

for tasks like housework, yard work, or taxes. Maybe you can hire out help for other things as well. It is worth looking at the things that take your time, and don't necessarily need to be done by you. At the same time, lots of people hire out childcare and I think this should be the last thing hired out. Sure, it is easy to get someone to watch the kids when other things need to get done, but the other things might not be more important.

I discovered the best description of our hectic schedules fall-out in Kim John Payne's book, *Simplicity Parenting*. He called it "soul fever." His book is about kids, but kids aren't the only ones who suffer. Soul fever is a sickness of the soul. It is when life gets too crazy, too stressed, and the emotions start getting affected. The symptoms are different for different people, just like a physical flu affects people differently. What the author said was that personality quirks come to the surface as symptoms. People may become extremely social or they may withdraw. They may give up or they may develop OCD (obsessive-compulsive disorder). The common theme is that with soul fever a person just isn't him or herself. The stress level is too high, and the soul is beginning to suffer.

There is hope. Easily enough, the treatment for soul fever is the same as a physical fever. Rest, cancel everything, don't go to work, stay away from others for a while, and just pamper yourself. That sounds like a great prescription, doesn't it?

Maybe you are experiencing soul fever now. Unknown to me then, soul fever is what pushed me to make the changes in my life to adopt minimalism and simplicity. I just couldn't keep up with everything. I was not who I wanted to be to anyone in my life and I felt stretched too thin. It isn't weakness, it is humanity. I can only do so many things and be in so many places before it starts going against the laws of physics (and in my body, the laws of nature). Knowing what I can do, doing what makes the greatest difference, and doing nothing else, is true mastery of time.

The goal here isn't time management any more than it is organizing stuff. The goal is to figure out how much time you can, or need to, cut out of the list and just leave as open space. The goal is space. Can you catch the running theme? Space and light.

Drawing the Circle in the Sand

A big part of freeing up our time is understanding boundaries. I have had mixed feelings with the concept of boundaries in the past because I feel that sometimes they can be misused. I believe an unbalanced understanding of, and use of, boundaries can damage self and relationships. The goal of boundaries isn't protection, but growth. We need each other, but we need to be able to control what and who we allow in.

To get and live an intentional life, boundaries need to be drawn around myself, my family, and my passion. With these boundaries in balance, I can guard against the unnecessary and negative, to allow growth and peace.

Myself

I need to have time to take care of myself. I need to set limits on what I can and can't do, and I need to pamper myself a bit. Learning these two ideas take time, and it is important time. I somehow grew up with the idea that time spent on myself was selfish and that all my time and energy should be focused outward. This isn't right. It doesn't work. Knowing I need personal time and boundaries is one thing, but actually making time, and then taking the time, is not always easy. The mind is a crazy thing. It can know I need to take care of myself but still feel it is selfish under the surface, making it hard not to feel guilty when I set my personal boundaries.

How can you make boundaries for yourself?

Go with your personality. Do you need a quiet hour in the evening with a book or a night out with friends to unwind? Do you need to run or eat chocolate? This is personal, but it is important to discover. I am not really a social person. I need quiet time to soak in the tub and read a book. I also discovered that I love writing. These are things I do for myself that help me pull away from all the craziness.

I set times and stick to them, just like I would a regular appointment. You can too. This is just as important, and should be treated as such. I have times in my day with the kids that are for them, and times that are for me. After lunch, they have a school break, and it is mommy's time. Then, in the afternoon, while they rest, I have mommy time again. Again, after they are put to bed, I have time for myself. This isn't time that I clean or do laundry; this is time when I can relax or work on my passion (more on that later). Having time that is mine makes it easier for me to give all of the rest of my time to them.

Family

It is so important to draw boundaries around the family. If you have kids, they might not yet realize that they need boundaries. They are learning and growing and the goal is to protect them from getting too overloaded. That is what we do as parents—teach and protect—because they aren't born knowing this stuff.

How does this work out?

As mentioned before in the time section, set a number of nights that family members can be gone and guard the ones left as family time. Even if it is working on a house project, it is together. There also needs to be nights where nothing is planned—including work. Depending on your family, the days and schedule can be different but, as a parent, it's your job to figure out what works best for your family and stick to it.

Have a family policy to stick up for each other. The world is a rough place and everybody needs to learn how to deal with it. But family is a place where the realities of the world don't need to be felt with the same sting. Family is a team. When one celebrates, everyone celebrates. When one succeeds, everyone succeeds. And if one is hurt or fails, all feel and cushion it together. Family was made because we needed it. The world isn't a perfect place and many families don't have this safe place, but for me (and for you), let's do our part for our families.

Passion

Protect your passion. This is a different concept that isn't talked about as much as it should be. Everyone has talents and dreams. I believe everyone has the potential to give something valuable to the world. With the necessity to make more and more money (to buy more and more stuff), these passions are often pushed to the side and never nurtured to the point where they could be considered valuable.

There are lots of business books now that talk about how you need to "do what you love." This is the same kind of concept, except I'm talking about something you might not ever be able to make a living doing. This passion is something that energizes you, something that refreshes you, something that you can think, do, and talk about, for hours without seeming to get tired. Do you know what your passion is? If not, this is a great personal exploration. Try out different things, study, and explore. I think it is possible to have lots of different passions at different times in your life.

I was never good at writing and I hated it in school. I started a website last year for my husband, trying to promote his photography and help him look more professional as a photographer, and I found that I really liked figuring it all out. I now have a blog that I spend a good chunk of my free time on and I love it. Come check it out at lovingsimpleliving.com. I would have never dreamed of doing website design or writing even an article, but now I am excited to give a book a chance. Sure, I hope it makes money, but that is not why I do it. I do it because I love it; it feeds me, and I believe it has something to offer others. I'm excited about what I can share with you because it has made such a difference in my life!

I also love music and have played guitar since high school. Just recently I started piano—I love it! I will never be a professional musician, but it feeds me, relaxes me, and makes me happy.

My husband was never creative in school, either. Really, we are both concrete people. We need answers to be right and grades to be certain. So, because of the way the school system is, mixed with our competitive spirit, we never enjoyed the creative subjects. Just in the past few years my husband has taken up photography and I'm amazed at how quickly his skills have developed. (As a shameless plug for my hubby—his website is bryonlippincott.com and it is amazing).

I share these personal experiences, but I'm sure you know many more people with all kinds of talent that they have discovered, fed, and explored. The thing is that doing something you love is way more efficient than doing something you aren't drawn to. It is a main point stressed in Marcus Buckingham's writings. I recommend his books if you are wanting to explore this area of passions more. I have read four of his books and I love his perspective. He talks about strengths as being something you are naturally good at and enjoy. Growing these areas in our lives is much easier than working on fixing areas we are weak in. So guard your passions. Find them, feed them, enjoy them, and share them.

How can we set up boundaries that will protect ourselves, our families, and our passions and not let other things creep in and take our time and energy? Learning to say "NO." Can you hear it? This is what minimalism sounds like. (Really, it is so we can say "Yes" to what we want, but it often comes after a lot of "noes.") It is important to leave it at "no" or one of the statements below. There is no need to explain or excuse yourself; this leaves room open for discussion and you might lose. Try some of the following, and then change the subject.

- ☐ "No, I don't think we will be able to this year/week/season."
- ☐ "I am so sorry, but it isn't going to work out."
- ☐ "Thanks, but no. We don't have time in our schedule for it right now."
- ☐ "I am flattered that you would consider/invite me. The idea sounds great, but I can't say yes this time."

If you are asked something that you would like to be involved in, take time to think it over. I have trouble with this sometimes. Really, I enjoy being in the middle of lots of different projects, but I often end up taking on too much. Try something like this:

- ☐ "That sounds really great, let me think it over."
- ☐ "Wow, I think we would really enjoy that; let me talk to the family and get back to you."

This goes for time commitments, responsibilities, and even social engagements. Thinking about it and talking to the other members of the family helps to keep you from constantly getting overextended.

The time exercise and the boundaries principles are great to talk about and create, but it is the day-to-day execution that determines if they will succeed or fail. Think on it and talk it over. Find ways to help yourself (and each other) stay accountable.

Okay, let's keep simplifying your life!

Money

Money is a simple thing. We all agree to believe in its value and we trade it around. But how and why does this simple thing become such a powerful force in our lives and often our biggest stressor? Somehow it ends up defining us and creating our lifestyle, instead of just being a tool for it. People buy the biggest house they can afford, the best cars they can afford, the nicest clothes they can afford, the fanciest vacations they can afford. Why is what we can afford the deciding factor for what we want? "Bigger," "faster," "farther," isn't always better; and it doesn't have to be what I want.

Society and especially commercial companies want us to believe that money = success. It doesn't. Let's just start here.

Money doesn't equal success.
Money doesn't define who I am.

If I can internalize and live the idea that "bigger and more doesn't equal better or success," it opens up a whole new world where I am freed from the chains of money.

Sure, money is necessary, and I like it a lot, but it is still simple.

1. I want X.

2. X costs Y.

3. I either have Y, or I need to save up to Y to get X.

Kids understand this concept. Simple, right? Where it gets more complicated is when we introduce debt and go against these simple rules.

Debt is the enemy! Let this be super, super, super clear. Bad, dangerous, deadly, trapping, and all other things evil. Debt = pain and stress (i.e., the opposite of simple). Debt comes when the "X and Y" simple-money concept is broken. The consequences are bad.

I love Dave Ramsey's Financial Freedom course and highly recommend it to people who want a simple, easy-to-follow financial path. He compares us and debt to a gazelle running away from a cheetah. Debt makes businesses big money, and they do everything they can to get you into debt so they can feed off you. Bad news! Run!

Don't Get into Debt and Do Everything You Can to Get out of Debt. Period.

With the moneybags and big-brains of our society partnering with businesses to study how they can advertise to get us to spend, this is definitely not an area where simple is easy. Don't get the two mixed up.

- ☐ Simple = knowing exactly what you should do, in what order, and with what tools
- ☐ Easy = not requiring effort

Simple money is *not* easy, but it is very rewarding.

Back when you dreamed in the introduction about how you wanted your life to be, I'm going to guess it didn't include money stress or money fights. So stand up and fight back against this demon! Money will work for you instead of you working for it!

Ready to deal with money the same way we did with our stuff and our time? First, you need two groups to be corralled and dissected:

- ☐ Money coming in
- ☐ Money going out

There is no way you can get a handle on your money without knowing these two things intimately. The goal is to make sure that "money in" is greater than "money out." Simple stuff, right? Some questions I hear are:

- ☐ Do I need to budget?
- ☐ Should I use only cash?
- ☐ What about putting money into savings at the beginning of the month?

There are lots of different money-management methods out there, and great books to go with them. I think that these are probably personal or couple-specific decisions because everyone is different, but stick to the goal of more money in than money out and do whatever plan will get you there. If the first idea or plan isn't working, try something else until you figure out a plan that works for you.

My husband and I keep a budget, but it looks different with self-employment income. I love the freedom of self-employment and think people should try it, but it has the downfall of not knowing what we will make in a month, or if we will make anything. Because of this it's hard to know what we should set our budget at. Our love is travel and we want to be able to take as much time off as possible for it. So what we have done is cut back our budget to be as small as possible so we can usually comfortably come in below our income. Then we put the rest in savings for travel. Save up and travel, save up and travel, has been our money plan because that is what we love as a family. Living on one income so I can stay home with the kids and living on as little as possible isn't for everyone. We follow the rules of "money in" and "money out" and we spend our money on what we love, so it works perfectly for us.

Let's see if we can work on widening the gap between the incoming and outgoing. Lots of this is basic, but it is worth looking at again. Here are some ideas:

Incoming

- ☐ Instead of just extra hours with a current job, is there room for advancement?
- ☐ What about a job change that might have better pay?
- ☐ Would additional education bring more pay in your field?
- ☐ Is there a way to build your passions into some additional income?

Outgoing

People tend to focus on one or the other, but both incoming and outgoing are important to master. Sometimes there is an undiscovered gem in outgoing.

There are those who barely make ends meet, but there are many more who "think" they only make ends meet, because of how they spend their money. Let's take a look at what we actually need: shelter, food, water, and clothes. In the world today, most first world countries have governments that provide or help with these four things if people run into trouble. I am all about helping people out and I am glad for these systems. There is also a large part of the world where people don't have these programs when they run into trouble. These people are the ones who barely make ends meet and have genuine money stress. True money stress shouldn't come from anyone when these four needs are met.

A large portion of our money is spent on things we want to have. This is really a freeing concept. Money is a choice; I choose where it goes.

Take a good hard look at the "out money." Do you like where it all goes? Do you get enjoyment from where it all goes? If not, cut it out just like the extra stuff that wasn't worth its space in **part 3**. I don't want to make this sound easy; it isn't. Just remember, you are in control, unless you are in debt. Debt is out of control and that is why it is the biggest enemy. Stay in control of your outgoing money. Hopefully by now, in this book, you have already made some cuts that save you money:

- ☐ Gotten rid of stuff (made money from the selling and don't have to pay to continue to maintain)
- ☐ Stopped getting stuff
- ☐ Maybe shrunk your living space which could lead to cheaper housing and should lead to cheaper utility bills
- ☐ Fewer time commitments saving gas and other fees

This isn't a money book; it is a simplicity book. But, excitingly, they can often go hand in hand.

Have you reached money simplicity through these steps? If not, keep cutting so you can pay off debt or make sure that incoming is more than outgoing. Keep working on it! It might be painful for a bit with some really harsh cutting, but it is worth it!

If you've freed up some extra money, sweet! That's a great position to be in. Look for ways to spend it that support a simple, minimalist lifestyle and your circles of yourself, your family, and your passions.

Electronics

Electronics have filled in the spot in our lives of can't-live-with-them and can't-live-without-them. Somehow, over the past several years, they have taken over our lives, our money, and our time more than they ever should. Just like money, electronics should never be in that spot. They were created to help us, not to rule over us.

This really hit home to me as I was trying to prioritize my time and life. I noticed that if the phone rang when I was reading or talking to my kids, I would automatically stop what I was doing and run for the phone. Do you do that, too? That felt wrong to me, and I have made an effort to stop. Electronics seem to demand attention no matter what else is going on. Why do they deserve it?

I have tried to do much better on this. For the record, I answer the phone for our businesses and when it rings it could be a customer (but, more likely, it is a telemarketer). Now, if the phone rings and I am in the middle of something with the kids, I let it go to voice mail. I can usually respond within ten or fifteen minutes if necessary. I hope this gives my kids a good example. I sure don't want them thinking that the stranger on the phone is more important than they are or more important than what we are working on.

With texting used constantly now there is definitely a window of thirty minutes to a few hours as an acceptable response time. Consider turning off alert sounds, at least for most people or apps, so they don't interrupt what you are working on.

I am working on scheduling my blogging and email time to once a day. Nothing is so urgent that it can't be dealt with in twenty-four hours. Facebook and other social networking sites can steal so much time. This is a personal thing, but with technology I try (and recommend) keeping them in this order.

1. Work (the necessary, in the allotted time)

2. Renewal (the boundary time for yourself, your family, and your passions)

3. Electronic fuzz like roaming social networks, Internet, or TV. This does not count for personal relaxation. Watching TV isn't always the best way to relax.

Electronics, like TV and Internet, are very addicting because they don't require much thought or effort. It is often just the easiest thing to do at the time, and human nature goes toward it for that reason.

Not new to our family, but a crazy concept to most people, is that we don't watch TV. In fact, we don't even have one. If the kids want to watch a DVD they watch it on the computer, but we don't even do that very often.

What is crazy to me is that the average American spends four hours and forty-nine minutes a day watching TV, and the average household spends eight hours and twenty-one minutes per day.

I read a book a few years ago called *The Other 8 Hours*. The idea was that we sleep for eight hours, work for eight hours, and have the other eight as the only real time we can control. The author didn't seem to take into account travel time, eating time, and cleaning time that take away from that eight hours. How, then, do people spend almost five hours in front of the TV? That is taking the last available minutes of their life and giving them away too! This is the time that we should have control over, to invest in ourselves, our family, and our passions.

Depressingly, this isn't the full picture. TV is also where we get the most brainwashed by marketing. TV is where we get the idea that we should be able to eat and spend more and more, leaving people dealing with a conflict of weight obsession and financial strain. Then these lies end up sucking so much time, energy, and happiness out of people. This isn't the only place where marketing targets people, but it is a major one.

So, turn it off! Get rid of it, especially the extra ones all over the house. Get back your life with the hours that you have control over.

Our process to cut down on TV-watching was slow. First, it was in the basement where it was too cold to sit for long in the winter. I also got frustrated with the scary commercials that would play when the kids were watching. Slowly, between having other things to do and not wanting our kids to see what the TV was showing, we watched less and less. When we actually got rid of it, it wasn't that big of a deal. Sure, I can't talk intelligently about the latest shows, but there are other things I would much rather talk about.

Having the computer allows for small bits of news coverage. If a huge earthquake happens or war breaks out, CNN or Facebook will tell me about it. But, for the most part, news is just news. I can't do anything about it, and it doesn't really affect me. I care about what happens, and I am sad the world is full of terribleness, but me watching and hearing about it every day doesn't do me, or others, any good.

I think lots of people go to TV as an escape. Whether an escape from pain, from making tough decisions, from guilt, or from something else. This isn't a long-term plan for life, health, or simplicity.

TV just steals time and time is the most important resource we have. I can find more money if I work hard enough, but I can't find more time.

I am so glad that we said "NO" to TV and got our time back.

Simplify Sound

This one isn't always thought of, but along with electronics comes an almost constant stream of noise. All noise is additional information that our brains need to process:

- ☐ TV on in the house
- ☐ Radio playing in the car
- ☐ Background music in stores
- ☐ Hold music on the phone
- ☐ Phones beeping to notify us of all kinds of life-changing events (e.g., a new email or tweet)
- ☐ Even unnecessary conversation

Cutting extra noise out as much as possible is an easy way to limit the extra information in our lives. I love music, but it is often too much to listen to music, listen to the kids, and plan lunch. After getting rid of the TV in our house we have grown to like silence and rarely play music. This may be because our kids create so much sound stimulation at such large volumes that we don't have room for more.

Most of us live in noisy worlds most of the day. What if our home was quiet as well as clean and simple? Quiet, just like space, is made to sit, savor, and enjoy.

On the Plate and Under the Skin

Simple health . . . okay, stop laughing. Really, I believe these two words can go together. We have spent time and pages already in this book on creating a space and life that is simple, but it would be a waste if we didn't have the health to enjoy it.

What's crazy is that most people know what they need to do to be healthy, but they don't do it. This has created a huge market for health information that sounds easy but often isn't based in science and often doesn't work. Just like the rest of this book, we aren't looking for easy. We are looking for simple and effective. I have this section after a bunch of the cutting out, because this may add time initially for some people. For example, if you don't already exercise and you have cut some other stuff out, exercise probably needs to be put into the schedule as something you need to do for yourself.

I wanted to share the basic principles from a program I like called NEWSTART (newstart.com). I love how this program is presented. It is so clear, complete, and simple. For simple health, you need:

- ☐ N—Nutrition
- ☐ E—Exercise
- ☐ W—Water
- ☐ S—Sunlight
- ☐ T—Temperance
- ☐ A—Air (fresh)
- ☐ R—Rest
- ☐ T—Trust in divine power

They have lots more resources at their website and have a great program that teaches and supports these areas. Most of us (hopefully) haven't gotten to the point where health is gone; it is just not always appreciated and guarded as well as it should be.

I struggle with getting fresh air and sunlight in the wintertime. I hate the cold. I also struggle with exercising regularly, but I am working on it and bringing my health goals down to this list definitely makes it simpler.

Many people find nutrition the most complicated. Simple food is something I love to study, talk about, and share on my blog. Maybe it is just because I love food! I believe that on this list (the NEWSTART list above) food is the place where our culture has gone the craziest for two reasons:

1. There are millions of books and places that tell people what to eat and what not to eat.

2. More and more of our food is more and more processed.

These two factors make food a huge stressor for people when it was meant to be enjoyed and bring life! I want food to be like my apartment: Simple, filled with what I love (nothing else), and inviting.

The best whole-picture perspective I have found is *In Defense of Food* by Michael Pollan. He coined the phrase, "Eat food, not too much, mostly plants." Food, in this phrase, means real food that hasn't been processed, altered, or added to.

Now, as easy as this sounds, finding "food" is getting harder and harder. Unfortunately, our society has sped up to the point of not having time to cook, and people feel forced to consume processed foods. Why do we think we are so busy we can't even cook our own food? Why do we think that healthy food is too expensive? Food is life. For most of time and in most of the world, food takes a much bigger percentage of time and money. The fact that cooking takes time and food costs money shouldn't be surprising or much of an argument. Food is pretty important.

Still, I Wanted to Address These Two Concerns:

☐ **Time**—I believe that simple health and simple food require cooking at home (or having a personal chef, but not many of us are financially there yet). But maybe our meals don't need to be as complicated as we think. They don't need to be made from a fancy recipe with strange ingredients and sit in the oven for an hour while leaving the kitchen a disaster. Sure, a simple meal won't compete with the fancy processed or restaurant meals, but maybe it doesn't need to. Fresh bread, olives, popcorn, fruit, salads, nuts, and other simple ingredients can make up a meal. Rather than making sure each meal is nutritionally balanced, you can look at the day as a whole. With meals and snacks it is still possible to get lots of balance without feeling like each meal needs to be a fancy spread.

☐ **Money**—People often believe that their food costs will go up if they try to eat whole, healthy food. I haven't found that to be the case. If you want to buy the fancy processed health food, that will be expensive. But the basics of rice or other grains, beans/legumes, fruit, and veggies (in season) as staples to the diet, and other things only as extras, comes out much easier on the budget.

What about Cravings?

Just cook it yourself and don't stress so much. I love making homemade fries or cinnamon buns sometimes. Making it at home means:

☐ **Fresher ingredients, no preservatives.** Also, it's hard to dump that much sugar or oil into something you're going to eat and it is easier to cut down or substitute something better. Seeing how it is made helps put it into perspective.

- ☐ **Less often.** The time and planning it takes don't happen nearly as often as the craving might be given into by something prepackaged.

With simplifying your food, hopefully, you can simplify your kitchen even more. Sure, we need variety in our diets, but the typical kitchen is packed with food that often sits for months or years without being eaten. That is too much variety.

Figure out what basic foods your family eats and stick to them when you organize and shop. I have found that planning out a general guideline for the week makes it easier to plan as well as shop with variety and simplicity. This is our current dinner plan. We don't always follow it and do move stuff around when we get an idea, but this provides a guideline, and when I shop I make sure we have the staples in the house. For lunch, we usually eat leftovers.

- ☐ Sunday—Soup
- ☐ Monday—Beans
- ☐ Tuesday—Rice
- ☐ Wednesday—Pasta
- ☐ Thursday—Potatoes
- ☐ Friday—Pizza
- ☐ Saturday—Unplanned

All these meals are pretty cheap (we make our own pizza crust) and are fairly quick and simple. I have lots more meal ideas and recipes on my blog.

Questions

Being without a TV seems a bit extreme, doesn't it?

I am not saying that it is necessary for simple living to be without a TV, but more and more subcultures and groups are talking about giving it up. Religious groups, parenting circles, and followers of minimalism all talk about reducing or getting rid of TV.

If you are going to have a TV, make sure what you are watching is intentional. One thing I read on *The Minimalists* website (theminimalists.com) suggested scheduling viewing at least twenty-four hours in advance and setting a cap on the week. This eliminates just sitting down and throwing the evening away merely out of habit.

Should I cancel my Facebook page or other social profiles?

Is it adding or taking away from your "simple life"? I love my social networking because it helps my book sales and blog, and it helps me connect with people easily. I have turned off all notifications, so I don't get phone beeps or emails every time something happens, and I don't often scroll through and roam the sites. All the different sites have a great way of checking to see if there is anything written to or about you, as well as a chance to add content, all right at the top or first screen.

I don't do games or any other add-ons and block them when I can. You also don't have to be friends with or connected to everyone you've ever met, either. It is fine to cut back to just people you want to be connected to. I don't think any of the networks notify the person being dropped from your list, so if you never talk to them, they will probably never notice or care.

Email is another thing people get carried away with checking all day, and it is pretty hard to live without it in our current society. So with email and any social profiles, it's a matter of deciding what and how much time you will give them.

What if I don't like healthy food and can't cook?

Healthy food isn't going to taste like unhealthy food. It just doesn't work that way. There are lots of different flavors and ways to cook whole foods. So experiment and practice. A kid needs to try a new food between five and ten times before they like it. Liking something has a lot to do with familiarity. With adults, because we change so slowly, it might take more time.

Simple recipes, simple tools. This isn't fancy French cooking or anything. Also, using simple foods that don't require cooking is a great option if you don't feel comfortable, or haven't as much time to cook.

1.

Self

First, we clear our physical space and fill it with only things we need and love. Next, we take action to clear out and make intentional our day-to-day lives. Now, we are going to look deeper into the mind. How we think, how we feel, and how that affects peace of mind. Society and sin in our world affect all levels. I believe this is the most important level, but it is probably the hardest to figure out and the hardest to work on. The other levels are important first because they give us the time to think and spend with ourselves to realize the amount of crazy that is left on this inner level.

I am a Christian and believe that God is the best one to help heal and teach me on this level. I feel I have been led in my simplicity journey from the start. I am excited to share with you what I have been taught and give God the credit for it. I believe God helps us simplify so we can realize we need His help on the inside. The world is a crazy place. Lives are never perfect. We are shaped and scarred, all in different ways, and we all struggle with these wounds.

I would love to say that I have my life completely figured out, but I don't. I can tell you that I love my little apartment and that it now has what I want in it. I have done pretty well working through **part 2** and am really happy with the results. It is this, **part 1**, that is the stuff that sits deep and is hard to clear out. This is stuff I am learning, struggling, and praying through. This is the stuff which, if given the time, space, and silence, comes creeping out to throw confusion around in our heads in what looks to others like a peaceful life.

I don't mean to make it sound terrible or frightening. This is the part that can make the biggest difference. The other parts are needed first, but it takes this final piece to experience true happiness.

The World as We Know It

How do we see the world? I believe there is absolute truth out there about what the world is, but seriously, we are not anywhere close to finding it. Everything we know, or think we know, is always, or probably will soon be, proven wrong. How many times has science changed its "facts" through history? All we ever know "for sure" is a current opinion. This is what we are working with in science, in parenting, in religion, and all other aspects of our lives. It is very important to understand this "fact"—that we don't know the true facts—in these areas, but I want to go deeper in the social aspect of it and see how it affects our lives.

It is human nature to judge by first impressions. There are tons of books and articles on how to create good impressions at interviews, blind or first dates, and even just how to dress and act every day so that people will get a good impression of me, pay me more, or think I am simply fabulous. There are tons of books because making a wrong impression happens so easily. There is some wonderful truth in all this self-help advice, but I wanted to tackle the other side of it—cataloging our first impressions of others.

Everyone is very different in personality, history, and even past hurts. We use these pieces of us, and other things, as "glasses" through which we create our first impressions of others. Some people I feel I will love right away and some just repel me. I'm a woman who is very concerned about my children's protection; I trust my intuition about some people and keep my kids away from them.

I want to talk about all the people in between and I want to suggest that you and I will benefit from dumping people into the first group (love) more often than the second (repel).

I'm sure you know people who are leery of everyone, who question everyone's motives, who are distrusting, and believe the world is out to get them. Their world is dark, about to end, and everyone is in it together against them. They see everyone as selfish and trying to manipulate them to get something. These people are miserable and stressful to be around.

I find it much easier to detect this in other people than in myself. Seeing it in other people recently, in how I've been judged on very minimal first impressions, has reminded me to take a hard look at myself and question how I judge others when I really know very little about them.

Maybe my motivation is selfish, but if the world I live in is largely created in my own mind, the "Is the glass half full or half empty?" mindset determines a huge part of my known reality. First impressions are important, but where are they coming from? I have seen, or given myself, negative first impressions based on:

- [ ] Name
- [ ] Friends
- [ ] Clothes
- [ ] Facial expression
- [ ] Location
- [ ] Skin color
- [ ] Marital status
- [ ] A few overheard words
- [ ] Nationality
- [ ] Kids' behavior
- [ ] Present company

. . . and probably lots more. What if, given only these superficial bits of information, I thought the best of them instead of the worst?

This is a simple tip more than a "global fuzzy" to make everyone think the best of everyone else (not that I am against that either). I am going at this for a practical, possibly selfish, reason. I can't change others in order to simplify my life, but I can change the way I see them, and in turn, create a much simpler and better life. There is value in surrounding oneself with friends who are supportive and positive, but part of this might be fixing our own eyes and perspective, before we try to fix others.

Can you change some of your social and relational realities by changing yourself? Yep. And if so, the saying that you can't change other people might, almost, in part, be wrong.

Window to the World

A second step for changing our reality is thankful thinking. So minimalism, or simple living, is having less stuff, right? Society tries very hard to make us feel like we don't have enough stuff and tries to make us want to buy more and more. This isn't evil—it makes tons of economic sense—I just don't believe it or want to follow it.

Life isn't perfect. It would be great if life were fair and there were ways to guarantee health and longevity, but there aren't. It's easy to get very upset over loss of these things, but because we are not in control, we don't really "own" anything we have. At any moment, people could leave our lives, our stuff could get destroyed, or our health could fail us. That's what life is like. Unfortunately, that is normal.

To really understand and be at peace with our lack of control and ownership is to be thankful. Every day I am given life, every moment I have loved ones around, every moment I experience health and safety, these moments are gifts I don't deserve.

This perspective is so important, but doesn't come naturally or easily. We are born wanting more. On top of that, lots of really smart people spend lots of money to strengthen the wanting tendency. Society, and even the government, wants us to spend, spend, spend. They want us to think that what we have is not enough, it is not complete, and that we need more, bigger, better. This desire isn't something to feel terrible or guilty about. It's part of being human, and it's made harder and harder by society. But thankfulness is still a choice. We can choose to be thankful.

I made another list (I love lists), and encourage you to make your own. This can go with the time and boundary notes. Write a list of the gifts you can be thankful for today. It is great to think about it, but it makes a big difference to actually write it out.

So, go get the pen and paper again.

Here Is My List. I Am Thankful For:

1. Life, all thirty-two years

2. Health

3. An amazing husband who is teaching me how to love and that I am valued

4. Energetic, healthy, and smart kids

5. The chance to stay home with my kids and teach them

6. Enough money in the bank to not worry about buying groceries

7. Being out of debt! Thank you, Dave Ramsey

8. The ability to read and the incredible amount of books available

9. Modern medicine

10. Great friends

11. Coffee

12. Dark chocolate

13. Olives (okay, I should probably just put great food or this list could really get long)

14. Sunny days and a south-facing apartment

15. Mostly consistent work since we became self-employed more than four years ago

16. A God who loves me and has saved me

17. Our minimalism journey which makes it much easier to clean, find things, and/or move

18. Awesome garage sales, Craigslist, and Goodwill for cheap and easy stuff "trading"

19. Blogging, the fun people I have gotten to know through it, and the challenging process of learning how to do it

20. Sleep—my favorite hobby

21. British comedies

22. Full tummies

23. Early bedtimes and quiet evenings

24. Brown paper packages and whiskers on kittens

25. You, reading this book! Writing a book has always been a dream of mine, and the fact that you are reading this is so exciting to me.

What does your list look like? Is your world starting to look a bit brighter and more spacious? I hope so! A great book that deals with this is *One Thousand Gifts* by Ann Voskamp. She also has an online community and Twitter feed where you can meet other people counting things they are thankful for. It's way nicer to be around people making these kinds of lists than people finding things wrong with the world. Be a thankful person with me.

The result of a thankful life is contentment. Doesn't that word just sound beautiful? Content. Sounds like the end of Thanksgiving dinner and lots of happy, full, relaxed, and refreshed feelings. I compare contentment with being a gift. It's a gift you can give yourself. The best kind of gift, the kind of gift that keeps on giving, and is always enough. Rest in it.

Digging Deeper

Now that the world looks a bit rosier, let's dig deeper in the closets of our lives for the "stuff" that is not necessary or beneficial. Let's look for stuff that gets in the way and trips us up as we lay in bed at night. Stuff that we try hard to keep hidden in back rooms when company comes over, but the effort to keep it all put away neatly doesn't always work.

Just because I like to keep things in chronological order, let's start with the closet of the past.

The Past

The past is such a crazy thing. There is no arguing that it is done and gone, but it can still have so much power over our present and future. We hold it in our minds and, far too often, let it run our lives and make our decisions. There are two areas in the past that I fight with and see others struggling with.

Hurt

I prefer to talk about things like contentment and space, simple and bright. Just the mention of the word "hurt" brings feelings that drag me down. But it's very important to pull this all the way out of the closet. Hurt is a real thing, even if it happened in the past. The problem is, even though we may want to, it is so hard to get rid of and move beyond. Pull it out and get a good look at it. Size it up, think about it, process it.

I would love to say I have the secret to erase this, but I don't. I will say that pulling it out, seeing it in the open, and talking about it starts shrinking it. Admitting to myself that I didn't deserve the pain, but that living in this world doesn't let me be immune to it either, helps.

This might be something you can work through on your own; it might be something you can just pull out and dump in the trash. If so, great! The sooner you can be free of it, the sooner you'll enjoy a better quality of life. But it might be something you need professional help with and it might never completely go away. Either way, don't ignore it. Minimize it as much as you can and keep working on getting rid of it instead of hiding and hoarding it away. God, as our original creator, can help repair and re-create.

Guilt & Regret

Guilt is another moldy box stuck in the corner. It needs to be pulled out and assessed. None of this is easy, but this stuff is too heavy, bulky, and stinky to keep around. Only when you're free of it, will you realize how much of your energy it was sapping. It's completely worth the effort!

No one is perfect, but it doesn't do any good to talk about the fact that there are other people out there who are worse. The goal here is to become better. This guilt (and sometimes the pain it causes) can be an action item like exercise equipment. It is painful to use, but there can be change and life brought out of it. God offers to be the power behind this. He has the strength and wisdom to make good what was bad.

Where is the guilt coming from? Can you work to make things right? Is there something you can do to apologize or repair? Nothing can be undone, but that doesn't always mean it has to stay done. Maybe it is something you need to stop continuing to do.

- ☐ Can you avoid doing it again?
- ☐ Can you help others not make the same mistake?

Admitting the wrongs you've done requires that you throw out the need for a perfect appearance (really that should have been thrown out long before now). It is okay not to be perfect; it is normal. You can't change the past, but you can make a difference in the present, and affect the future.

Regret is the sibling of guilt. It's guilt mixed with sadness or grief over something you did or failed to do. Ask yourself:

☐ Can the thing be done now? If not, it just might need to be put in the trash pile.

Now let's move beyond the past.

The Present

Who Are You?

When I first quit my job about four years ago, I really struggled with identity. Not that I had a great job, but I was pretty proud of it and enjoyed it. When I met someone, or was introduced, I had an identity. I was Lorilee and I was a manager. After I quit, I was Lorilee, a stay-at-home mom. It just doesn't have the same ring to it no matter how much more I value it over my job and believe it is more important. And it shouldn't; a stay-at-home mom isn't my identity either. Mother, woman, wife, teacher, blogger. All these things tell about me, but they are not me. What makes me different?

It's kind of funny. I want to be "me" and "me" is someone who is different than anyone else. I want to be unique and special and not just any mom or wife. At the same time there is a need to fit in. Fitting in is often seen as being like everyone else. No wonder we have so much trouble with our identity. These two are polar opposites.

Fitting in, being accepted as part of the group because you are just like everyone else, or striving for being "normal" can't co-exist with being at peace with my true identity. This is a cover up for not feeling I have value.

You and I have value! God says so; He chose to make us. I want to share this with you from a book I read. The whole book is excellent, but this part jumped out at me. I changed the author's name to my name. You can change it to your name.

My name is *Lorilee Lippincott.* I am the chosen and adopted daughter of the Most High King. I'm the heir to an eternal inheritance waiting for me in heaven. I have been bought and completely paid for by the perfect sacrifice of Christ's own blood and am sealed throughout all eternity by God's Holy Spirit. Don't mess with me!

From *Spiritual Parenting*, by Michelle Anthony

That sounds good. It has power and kick. Read it again out loud, maybe a couple times, until it really sinks in. Don't mess with me!

When we go to other people, like friends, parents, or significant others, to verify our worth, we are doomed for failure. They didn't make you so they can't understand your true value. They are also human and are struggling to find their own value.

When we all try to pull our value from each other, it doesn't work. There is always more needing than there is giving and the pool of value becomes bankrupt. However, when your value comes from a higher source, if someone doesn't like you, it doesn't leave the same mark. Instead of questioning your value against their opinion, you can question their ability to evaluate value. You are valuable! Don't let that be questioned.

On this note, always remember that everyone else you are dealing with is also valuable. Out of this same value we have for ourselves and the self-respect it creates, we can find respect for others. Others deserve respect whether we like them or not, and whether they like us or not. People are valuable.

Once we can establish self-worth, we can begin evaluating the "stuff" piled in the self-expectation corner.

I really struggle with this. I'm an overachiever, perfectionist, and maximizer, and all these are good in some ways and I like these aspects of me most of the time. But, at the end of the day, these same things make it hard to remember that I am not defined by what I can get done or what I didn't get done.

It is often said, and it is very true, that we are hardest on ourselves. This can cause:

- ☐ Guilt
- ☐ Fear of trying
- ☐ Fear of failure
- ☐ Never being happy with something

This bad "stuff" does nothing to help with a new simple life and needs to be removed from the closet. Self-expectations, when seen as "who I want to be," can be used as motivators.

I really like the idea of a personal mission statement that Stephen R. Covey talked about in his book, *The 7 Habits of Highly Effective People.* It's a way of conveying what I am and what I plan to be. It's my vision. I've written out personal mission statements a few times in my life and I think they do a great job of clearing out the baggage of low self-worth and unrealistically high self-expectations.

In a personal mission statement, I can talk about what I value and how I plan to continue to value it. In a mission statement, my focus is on the clear, un-messy future instead of the incomplete present.

I would definitely recommend you take some time to write out a mission statement. It could be a line or two or a page or two, but write out who you are and who you are going to be. Set it somewhere where you can see it often or in a journal that is more private, but still accessible and opened often. If things don't go as planned, or things don't work out, that is part of life. Keep looking ahead, and keep doing what you can, to live up to the mission statement you created.

What about God? How Can I Live Up?

I think Christianity is full of people struggling to live up to religious expectations. This isn't biblical. Look at the heroes in the Bible. They weren't always stressing about if they were involved enough at church, if they were witnessing enough to others, or if they were living up to what they were taught. This isn't what was on their mind or in their writing. Looking at Jesus' life, it wasn't on His either. So, why do we stress about it so much? The heroes of the Bible and Jesus simply focused on God.

Expectations in Christianity point the focus in the wrong direction. Anywhere or anything that is focused on self is wrong. The only expectation in true Christianity is focusing on God. There is nothing crazy here, no balance to figure out. One thing, and one thing only, is to be our aim: God.

Look at the life of Christ. There was a whole world to preach to, heal, or pick as disciples. The opportunities and the task of showing the world God's love and plan could be incredibly overwhelming, but Christ wasn't overwhelmed by it. He never seemed to be in a hurry or worrying about what He wasn't getting done. He spent lots of time in prayer and did what His Father told him to do. In three and a half years He changed and saved the world.

So, don't get bogged down with everything you feel you have to do or be! Learn to love and value yourself, write a personal mission (vision) statement, and walk with Christ.

What is the last closet?

The Future—Shelf One

On the first shelf of the "future" closet, continuing with the idea of expectations and motivation, is our relationship with goals. I think goals are very important, but often they rob me of a simple life.

There is a minimalist idea out there about having no goals, and I have spent a bunch of time thinking about it. First, I liked the idea, but in practice I feel I rob myself to do away with them completely.

Instead of doing away with goals (this book is the product of a goal, and so is my blog) I want to turn the focus of my goals to the present. Sure, there will still be some long-range goals, but they will be secondary to my goals for the present.

Beyond that, all my goals will be movable targets. They will bend and re-adjust as necessary based on my present priorities. Meeting or not meeting goals will be a positive part of my life instead of a rush or guilt-push from behind. Goals need to be a positive motivator, not a stressor.

Traditionally, goals can be an enemy to living in the present. Instead of doing away with them, I will direct them toward my present situation. They will be an extension of my personal mission statement more than they will be measurable targets that are still far off in the future. Here's how I see it affecting my life and thinking.

Business

With our construction business, we learned very early on that we didn't want long-range goals. From the beginning, when we went into business over five years ago, we knew we didn't want to have employees. In society and business the rule is to start, grow, run well, and sell a business. That is just how it's supposed to be done. We never wanted that track because we didn't want to be tied down to the schedule and commitment needed for that kind of growth. We want our businesses to work for us and not the other way around. We work as much as we need to and not any more.

Since this has been our track, we have also been very flexible. We do work for ourselves and we do sub work for other contractors. We do residential, as well as commercial. We have been very blessed and (almost) always had work during the past four years, which have been very hard years for the construction business. Doing the job right, being honest, making friends, and trusting in God, have allowed us to live and work this way. These are present goals allowing our company to work for us instead of the other way around.

Kids and Homeschooling

I have been trying to figure out how to properly prepare my kids for life and college almost since they were born. But since listening to Ken Robinson's talks about how the current education system is not preparing kids for the future job world, I have been struggling with what to do. Instead of working on a goal that I can't understand (what my kids will actually need to be prepared for in the future) and a goal I can't control ('cause, best as I try, I still can't control my kids), I am going to work in the present on helping them develop their passions and develop a love of learning. Instead of focusing their whole childhood on teaching them to survive in the "real world," I can allow them to teach me how to enjoy the present.

Money

We do have money goals because we are saving to travel more as a family. This goal is very flexible as we are self-employed and don't know month-to-month how much money will come in. If I set up specific long-range goals it would set me up for lots of frustration from things I can't control. So, I spend as little as possible. We know what goal we are working toward and what we will do when we get there.

Self and Health

I want to develop the habit of making my personal growth and health a priority each day.

Relationally

In the time I am given each day, I want to make the habit of taking the time to show others that they are valuable.

Blog and Books

I do have goals with my blog and writing. I have goals on my output. I have the goal to get this book done and I have the goal to post quality content several times a week. I can generate good content, but the rest is largely out of my hands. Goals for readership or other measurable goals do not help my writing or my passion. Eternal destiny is shaped in the present and not in reaching a long-range goal.

The more I think about goals this way, the more I see the life of Christ like this. He had vision and a big long-range goal that He took very seriously. It was the purpose of His life. But, to achieve that, He didn't have goals for number of sermons, or enlarging His group of disciples or any other nice measurable target. These goals would have gotten in the way of relying on the Father and allowing the Father to lead Him. Goals like these would have been a distraction.

Living with lots of long-range goals seems to put "arriving" or happiness just out of reach. I tell myself, "when I reach this goal then..." Or, "I just need to work and get this done and then..." but one goal overlaps another goal and "then" never comes. What if "then" could be now, and could be every day, every minute?

I often think of people who are diagnosed with a terminal disease and have years or maybe months to live. The question always is "how would you live your life differently if you knew you only had ___ months, days, or years to live?" But this is silly. Terminal diagnoses or not, I don't know if I am going to live the next thirty seconds or not. I want to live each moment intentionally without putting it off for the future.

Living with present goals as my main focus means I can be fully accomplished every day. I can be fully accomplished right now. I can be right on time with my life instead of behind or ahead. And, really, right on time is all we ever can be with our lives.

The Future—Shelf Two

This second shelf drives me crazy. **The world is about to end!**

This seems to come from everywhere. There are medical scares, war scares, natural disaster scares, political scares, religious scares, and probably more. I don't disagree with any of it. I believe the world is hanging on by a thread and the Bible says it is going to end. However, thinking and trying to plan for it gets me nowhere. *Nowhere!*

The fact that the world is, will, or could end at any time or hundreds of years from now, is not something I can control. I can't do anything to stop how it will affect me. I don't understand people buying bunkers, storing food, or taking survival classes. To properly prepare one would need to know what was going to happen, so they could prepare for it. People can try and come up with what they think will happen, but they have no clue, so they can't prepare. There are too many different ways the world could blow up and each big disaster we have had on the planet is different than the last.

So, please clean this baggage out of your closets and be done with it. I hate the feeling in the pit of my stomach when someone starts going on about these possibilities. It isn't about ignoring facts or avoiding anything; it's about focusing on what matters, and what I can do. What fills my life and my space in the present is what I can do something about and enjoy. The rest just sucks energy and time.

What does all the fear of the future matter if I get hit by a truck tomorrow? Not a thing. So all that time and stressing would be a waste anyway.

Religion seems to get hung up on this, at least some religious people do, arguing that it pulls people closer to God and scares them into taking Him seriously. I don't like this because fear isn't what God is about. I follow a God I want to run to and spend time with because of who He is and what He has done for me, not for personal safety or gain. I want to share this God with others.

In life there is always the ability to look at the future as a cup half empty or half full. There is a positive and negative side to everything. Because you are the one who controls your mind, you can choose what gets kept and what gets tossed. Choose to toss the negative, the stuff that drags you down. If you have learned anything from the book so far, it is that less good stuff is far better than a whole pile of junk. Less is better when it is specifically chosen to build up, grow, and enjoy.

The Future—Planning—Shelf Three

The third and final shelf in the future closet I wanted to talk about deals with excessive planning and anticipation. This is probably the hardest area for me to clean out. I find myself thinking in the future far too often. I am always planning future things in my head from writing projects, to reaching a money goal, to moving, or vacations. I struggle with this so badly that some days, when I need to come up with the day's date, I am sometimes a week or two ahead. I think planning is so important, but the present is reality. It is hard to enjoy present reality when the future always has a glowing picture of more and better. This steals contentment from the present.

In the past year we have been very close to several great opportunities that would have moved us around the country and the world. It has been very draining to work, pray, hope, and talk through these opportunities only to have them slowly slip away. It isn't all disappointment. I believe God is in control of what we are doing and where we are and I can see this as time continues on. What is hardest is the time and energy that planning, dreaming, and thinking about the options seem to steal from both my husband and me.

What my husband and I have agreed to do is to intentionally focus on the present and worry less about figuring out five or so different possible futures. I love that both of our personalities are always looking for new things and better opportunities for our family, but in looking for them, we need to wait until they are a reality before we spend the time and emotional energy processing and planning them.

Out of Body Simple

The last idea I wanted to talk about in simple and intentional living is giving. Initially, this sounds like adding when the focus of the book is cleaning out, but it doesn't have that end result. Whether you give time or money it has the opposite effect. When giving to others, I've found I worry and think about myself less. When giving to others, I realize how much I have and that I'm blessed. Also, just the fact that I'm giving makes me feel rich. I have more than I need and I can share it with others. That is abundance.

Giving is often the most efficient use of money. For example, twenty dollars doesn't even cover a dinner out for our family. If I invest twenty dollars at 12 percent (unlikely in the current economy), in ten years it will be about $65.00. If I give it away, that twenty dollars could go towards teaching one child to read and write. That child could break out of a cycle of poverty in ten years. Or it could provide chickens to a family. Those chickens could give hundreds or thousands of new chickens or eggs in ten years, saving the lives of children that might have died from starvation or helping a family have enough money from selling the extras to send their kids to school. How does that compare to a plate of pasta or an invested sixty-odd dollars? It isn't comparable.

Sure, I can't give all my money away, but the process of giving and being a part of making the above-mentioned miracles become a reality with some of my money is fun. It is a privilege, not a sacrifice. Giving and focusing on the good that can be done is a great way to:

- ☐ Worry less about what you don't have
- ☐ Stress less about how bad the world is
- ☐ Stop feeling helpless

We can't change the world, but we can change lives.

What we have found works for us is to agree that a specific percentage of our money will go to others. Some goes to the church, but lots of it is "play/pray money" to give where we find need. When we come across a need or an opportunity, we have a pool of money to draw from to help. For me, this is the most fun money to spend. Because we budget for it, before the money even hits the bank, it is easy to give whenever we see a cause we want to support.

Ever since we got married, I have tracked our net worth and the amount we've given at the end of each year. It is nothing fancy, just a spreadsheet that records our progress, but it's exciting to see how money we have consistently given away has added up. While I'm glad we got out of debt and invested, what I am really proud of is where we have invested in others. I want my life and my work to make a difference in this world. I am excited that my money can help change someone's life that I will probably never meet.

I challenge you, depending on where you are with finances, to set aside a specific amount or percentage of money each month to give away and start tracking it. This isn't a number to be shared around or bragged about. Ours is a secret between my husband and me. It is for our joy, peace of mind, and acting out our purpose.

Questions

How can I know which charities are going to use my money well?

I use charitynavigator.org. It is an organization that reviews charities from an independent and third-party perspective. It is easy to use and has lots of good information. I also like charities that have their financial records easily accessible on their website.

With so many needs in so many places all over the world, where can I get involved?

What needs or groups of people really connect with you? Though there is need everywhere, trying to solve all the world's problems quickly becomes overwhelming. Everyone is different. Go with your gut. What do you connect with the most? What issues bring out the biggest emotional response in you? Find ways to join in helping these causes and celebrate with their victories.

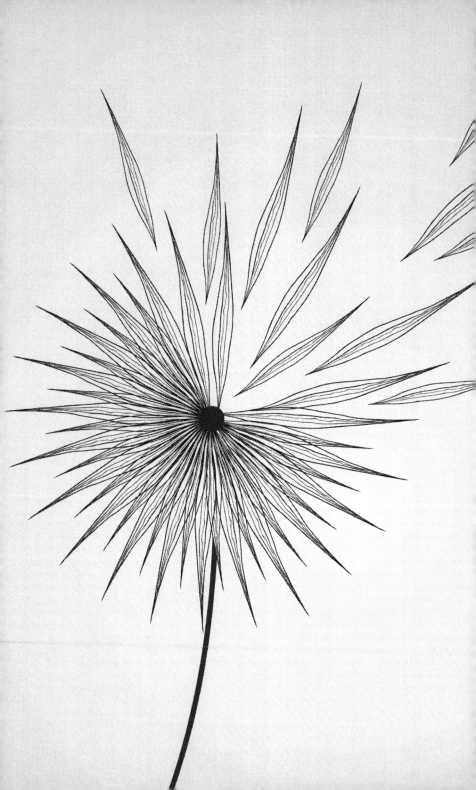

Stop.

Stop

Remember that picture we created in our minds at the beginning of the book? How does it compare to what you have created (or will create if you are reading this book straight through)? Is it close? Different? Better? Clearer? Has the work been hard? How long has it taken? How long do you think it will take? Get out the lists you have made through the book and review them. Tell other people about what you're working on, people who will help motivate you and keep you accountable.

I would love to say this book is about a journey with a clear destination, but it isn't. It is just about a journey. Really, that is what life is. When we get confused about life having a destination, we start living for reaching that destination, instead of enjoying and focusing on the journey.

Nature and God teach us through this fact every day as our body grows and dies. There is no great leap and then a plateau. Sure, there is more growth sometimes than others, but there is this balance of growing and dying down to the very cell level every second. The difference between our life and our body is that in our life we have a choice as to how much we grow or die each day. I believe God gives us only so long for our journey, but if we never really travel far, grow much, or learn much along the way, the time we are given seems like a waste.

So, there's no destination, but I believe that if we choose to grow and move farther along while making the best of the journey, our lives can get better and better. There is more to see, more to enjoy, more to understand, and better relationships.

The ideas and ideals in this book are countercultural. Most people don't do these things. Most people don't analyze their life enough to know they are choosing to follow society, instead of choosing the path that is right for them. I will not be one of those people. You bought and read through this book. You are not one of those people, either. Not that society or "normalcy" is bad; there is just more to life than the easy path.

I love the choices I have made for me and my family, but I still have a hard time telling others because I'm scared of what they might think of me. On the phone, if I have to give my address, just saying the apartment number is difficult. There is something so ingrained in me saying my importance as a human being is measured by where I live and what I own. Maybe I will be able to accept this and live it proudly or maybe I will always worry about being judged for how I live differently. Either way, I am glad I made the changes and I am excited for many more years of growing and changing based on what I am learning. This is living.

"The unexamined life is not worth living" was said by Socrates at his trial before he was put to death for questioning the societal norm. We are so privileged to live in an age and place where we have the freedom to think and act on it. We are so lucky to have this freedom, to have so much education, to have so many inspiring people to hear at the touch of a button or read about at the opening of a book. Now more than anything, we can't waste it.

Look closely at your life. Are you running around, trying to live up to everything you've been taught and society keeps preaching? It is a downward spiral. No matter how much money you can get, you will never be able to buy as much as you would like. No matter how much popularity you find, there will still be people who don't know or like you. No matter how much influence you gain, you will not be able to change people. No matter how much education you get, you will not find pure truth. It is a treadmill or a hamster wheel; it doesn't get anywhere and it isn't as fun as it looks.

The concepts in this book are not easy. I made that promise from the start. However, they're simple, sometimes painfully simple. It takes hard work, but the steps are clear.

We only have one life to live and in that life we have no idea how long we have. It isn't morbid to think about death; it is a reality we can't forget. Don't wait to start:

- ☐ Making your own choices
- ☐ Living your own life
- ☐ Making your priorities priority
- ☐ Working on your passion
- ☐ Healing past hurts
- ☐ Making past wrongs right
- ☐ Giving
- ☐ Serving
- ☐ Living!

Start today to make your journey the best it can be. It is your journey to enjoy! I am so excited for you!

My Journey

A few months after finishing this book we found a job teaching English to college students in a small city in China. We got plane tickets, visas, and gave away almost all of the rest of our stuff within a few weeks . . . and we left . . . and we have never looked back.

It was both terrifying and exciting. It is something we dreamed of being able to do from the time we started simplifying, but just like a lot of things worth doing, it was still scary. As far as living intentionally and creating our own life, we were doing it. As far as having things figured out and being sure we weren't making a huge mistake, we didn't have that.

When the first edition of this book was published, we had been in China for several months and I signed copies for my students. We owned only a few suitcases full of personal stuff and were deep in learning about another culture and growing as a family.

From there we were able to work more on our passions and hobbies and the following year started to work full time in the creative space for nonprofits and humanitarian organizations. Now, six years later, we are still working in nonprofit media and marketing and it really feels like living the dream.

After a few years living in China and working locally we got jobs in other parts of Asia. We spent a majority of the next two years traveling around Asia with our kids, limited to what we could put in backpacks (trains and subways are a terrible place to try and roll a suitcase).

This was definitely our most "minimalist" time. Most of our bags held our photo and video gear and lighting. We also had homeschool supplies and basic kitchen supplies for hotel living. It left painfully little space for clothes or anything extra. In both six-plus-month trips we covered cold and hot weather so clothes were minimal and strategic.

It was incredible. Most of our travel was over land by train (sometimes bus) and we got to see so much of the countries we visited. We also got to meet incredible people who are transforming their piece of the world.

After having our "home base" in China for two years, we decided to move to Cambodia because the cost of living and visa situation was much better. We mailed a few boxes over land and packed the rest of what we owned in backpacks.

However, one Sunday in September of 2016 I came down with a fever and got really sick. Over the week I just kept getting worse until we ended up calling an ambulance in the middle of the night the following Saturday.

I spent most of the next two and a half years in bed. At first I was unable to handle any sound and conversation was too much for me. My days were spent on a cot beside the bathroom so I only had a few steps to take. I played hours of solitaire silently on the iPad and the kids would come in at night to give me a hug.

Thankfully, I've regained a lot of strength and now can interact with my kids and do a few hours of work most days. I can handle small social situations and can get out in a wheelchair around town if the areas aren't too busy or loud.

At first, I was sure I was dying. I was struggling to breathe and couldn't feel my arms and legs. It was terrifying.

Once I was fully tested at the hospital and received a diagnosis for a chronic neurological disorder that wasn't life threatening, it became a new battle. What is this new life going to be like?

The stuff I wrote in this book, like always being thankful, living in the present, and not finding identity in what I do . . . all of it came back in haunting ways. Not only did I realize I found my value in my job, I also found it in my parenting, my determination, my work ethic, and my ability to help others. All of it was taken from me. For months at a time I was just taken care of and couldn't do anything but lay there.

Per all the lessons I had learned that I put in this book, it was like an intensive graduate program. My schedule was completely cleared for me. I didn't have to say "no" to anything because I could barely make it to the bathroom and back. All I had was time, and lots of it. I spent days and weeks going through past hurts and challenges I thought I had long ago dealt with. I struggled with what I believed and how to wrap my mind around a new uncertain reality.

It was all the same lessons, though—this illness is just a much harder teacher. I still have to learn to live in the present. I have to be very careful how I spend my time and energy because it is extremely limited. I definitely can't let stuff start collecting because I don't have the ability to maintain much. I am much healthier emotionally and physically when I can live with gratitude and focus on others.

My "simple life" just looks a lot different than I would have thought when I first wrote this book years ago.

We are also not living out of backpacks or suitcases anymore. It was a wonderful time and one I will always remember fondly, but my kids are now sixteen and thirteen years old, and they have desperately wanted their own rooms for the last few years.

We now live in Thailand where the medical care is much better than Cambodia. We have a small house with three bedrooms and way more space than we had when I first wrote this book. We still have a donate pile/place in the house that we are constantly filling up. However, simplifying is not a big piece of our lives any more. I hope it won't be for you after a few years. It just becomes a habit.

We spend our energies in other spaces we are passionate about. My husband and I (as my health allows) run a ministry called Sharing Dots (sharingdots.org) where we help nonprofits and humanitarian organizations with media and marketing. We love it. It isn't everyone's life, but we feel it is the one that fits us.

We could have never started on this wild journey without simplifying and taking the first scary steps to intentionally look at our lives and where we belonged. It might be simplistic to say getting rid of the first books off the shelf led to us living the life we do now, but it wouldn't be wrong either.

Good luck! I'm excited for you and your journey!

Ending Thoughts

I would love to hear your thoughts on this book and your story. Please come by my website at lovingsimple living.com and introduce yourself. I am not posting regularly on it currently but there are several years of posts and the contact page is still working.

You can also find me on Facebook: facebook.com /lovingsimpleliving

Acknowledgments

When I pick up a book, I don't usually pay much attention to the acknowledgments section, instead prioritizing the "real" content. They usually say things like "I could have never written the book without . . ." or "These people made this book possible," etc. Now, after writing my own book, I understand the truth in these statements. You are holding a book in your hands that would have never been finished without the help and kindness of many people.

Specifically, I want to thank my husband and my kids for their patience as I put so many hours into getting this project done. Also, I had great help editing from several friends (together they all created a totally new, easy-to-read book for you): Kari Halweg, AK Ross, Amy Tanner, and Kendra Carlson (and last-minute help from Shelly Pitford and Darrylin Lippincott). I also had invaluable encouragement from Jessy Carlson and Brenda Eidel.

I want to thank all the new friends I have made through blogging and on Twitter who have reviewed my book and encouraged my process.

Finally, I am so thankful for you reading this book. I would love to hear from you when you are done and get to know you more on the website or social media. Hope you enjoyed!

Index

A

active toys, 32
Anthony, Michelle, 115
art stuff, 31, 35

B

book basket, 34
books, 51
boundaries, 66
budget, 75–76
business, 120–121

C

calendar, 61–62
charities, 131
Christ, 118–119, 122–123
closet, 15–20
clothes, 15–20, 51
    dress-up, 32
Cohen, Felice, 41
construction toys, 31–32
cooking, 91–92, 96–97
Covey, Stephen R., 117
cravings, 92–94

D

debt, 74–79
delegating, 62–63

devices, 81–85, 87–88, 95–96
diet, 89–94, 96–97
dolls, 31
donation, 51
dress-up clothes, 32

E

education, 121
electronics, 81–85

F

Facebook, 95–96
families, 59–60, 67
first impressions, 103–105
food, 9, 23–25, 89–94, 96–97
furniture, 37–39
future, 119–120, 124–126

G

games, 32, 35
garage sale, 51–52
goals, 123
God, 101–102, 118–119
gratitude, 107–110
guilt, 113–114

H

health, 89–94, 122
home, 41–43

homeschooling, 121
horizontal spaces, 49
hours, work, 62
hurt, 112
husband, 52

I
identity, 114–118
impressions, 103–105
In Defense of Food (Pollan), 91

J
Johnson, Gregory Paul, 41

K
kitchen, 21–25

M
mail, 9
meals, 59–60
minimalism, 5–6
money, 73–79, 92, 121–122,
 127–128, 131

N
NEWSTART, 89–91
"No," 70–71
noise, 87–88
nutrition, 89–94, 96–97

O
One Thousand Gifts (Voskamp), 110

P
papers, 9
partner, 52
passion, 68–71
past, 112
Payne, Kim John, 33, 63
personality, 66
Pollan, Michael, 91

purchases, 9–11
*Put Your Life on a Diet: Lessons
 Learned from Living in 140
 Square Feet* (Johnson), 41
puzzles, 32, 35

R
regret, 113–114
religion, 101–102, 118–119
Robinson, Ken, 121

S
saying NO, 70–71
selling stuff, 51–52
*7 Habits of Highly Effective People,
 The* (Covey), 117
shelter, 41–43
Simplicity Parenting (Payne), 33, 63
social media, 95–96
Socrates, 137
soul fever, 63–64
sound, 87–88
space, 57–58
spending, 77–79
spirituality, 101–102, 118–119
Spiritual Parenting (Anthony), 115
stuff, 3–13, 45–47

T
television, 83–85, 95
texting, 82
time, 59–64, 91–92
toys, 27–35
TV, 83–85, 95

V
Voskamp, Ann, 110

W
wife, 52
work hours, 62

Made in the USA
Las Vegas, NV
14 February 2022